WASTING TIME ON THE INTERNET

KENNETH GOLDSMITH

HARPER PERENNIAL

NEW YORK • LONDON • TORONTO • SYDNEY • NEW DELHI • AUCKLAND

HARPER PERENNIAL

WASTING TIME ON THE INTERNET. Copyright © 2016 by
Kenneth Goldsmith. All rights reserved. Printed in the
United States of America. No part of this book may be used
or reproduced in any manner whatsoever without written
permission except in the case of brief quotations embodied in critical articles and reviews. For information, address
HarperCollins Publishers, 195 Broadway, New York, NY
10007.

HarperCollins books may be purchased for educational,
business, or sales promotional use. For information, please
e-mail the Special Markets Department at SPsales@harper
collins.com.

FIRST EDITION

Designed by Jamie Lynn Kerner

Library of Congress Cataloging-in-Publication Data has
been applied for.

ISBN 978-0-06-241647-6

16 17 18 19 20   RRD   10 9 8 7 6 5 4 3 2 1

For Finnegan and Cassius

CONTENTS

INTRODUCTION

Let's Get Lost

I'm wasting time on the Internet. I click to the *New York Times* front page to see the latest headlines and today a major nuclear deal with Iran was signed. The banner headline screams HISTORY and even though I haven't really been following the story, I click on it. I'm taken to a page with an embedded video that features Thomas Friedman asking Obama to explain what he thinks the United States gained from the nuclear deal with Iran. I check the time on the video—three and a half minutes—and figure that's not too long to listen to the president speak. He speaks; I watch. He continues to speak; I scroll through my Twitter feed but I still listen. I click back on the *Times* window and watch again. Somewhere about the three-minute mark, I start to think, Am I really wasting time on the Internet? This is important stuff that I've stumbled on to. I'm struggling to see what's so shameful about this. The video ends and, impressed by what the president was saying, I start to read Freidman's lengthy article about this beneath the video. I read the first few paragraphs carefully, then scroll down and read some more. It's starting to get too granular for me. But my interest is piqued. Although I'm not going to read this piece to the end, I'm going to start following this story as it unfurls over the next few days. I stumbled on it and got hooked. Is my engagement deep? Not right now. But judging by the way these things tend to go, as I start to follow the story, my appetite for the topic will most likely become voracious. I can't see this event—one that happens several times a day—as being anything other than good. Because of it, I'm better informed, more engaged, and perhaps even a bit smarter.

After I finish with this article, I click over to Facebook and find myself watching a video of Keith Richards discussing how he gets ideas for his songs. He says that when he's in restaurants and overhears conversation coming from the next table, he simply writes down what they're saying. "Give me a napkin and a pen," he says, smiling. "You feel that one phrase could be a song." Although the video is only a minute long, it's packed with wisdom. Really? Could his process be that simple, that pure? After listening to Keith, I feel inspired. After all, I feel like I spend tons of time eavesdropping on Facebook conversations. Might I be able to wring a song or a poem out of those as well?

I'm back on Facebook, and the next thing I know I'm looking at this incredible black-and-white photo from 1917 of a full-size battleship being built in New York's Union Square. The picture is huge and brimming with details. I click on it and I'm taken to a website. As I scroll down, there's a short explanatory text about how this came to be, followed by a dozen more giant, rich photos of the ship being built in progress. It's fascinating. I just wrote a book about New York City and I'm floored that I somehow missed this but grateful to know about it. I bookmark the page and move on.

What is wasting time on the Internet? It's not so easy to say. It strikes me that it can't be simply defined. When I was clicking around, was I wasting time because I should've been working instead? But I had spent hours working—in front of the same screen—and quite frankly I needed a break. I needed to stop thinking about work and do a bit of drifting. But, unlike the common perception of what we do when we waste time on the Internet, I wasn't watching cat videos—well, maybe one or two. I was actually interested in the things that I stumbled on: the president, the rock star, and the battleship. I had the choice not to click on these things, but I chose to do so. They seemed to me to be genuinely interesting. There were many more things that I didn't click on.

Listening to Internet pundits tell it, you'd think we stare for three hours at clickbait—those web pages with hypersensational headlines that beg you to click on them—the way we once sat down and watched three hours of cartoons on Saturday morning TV. But the truth is most of us don't do any one thing on the Internet for three hours. Instead, we do many things during that time, some of it frivolous, some of it heavy. Our time spent in front of the computer is a mixed time, a time that reflects our desires—as opposed to the glazed-eyed stare we got from sitting in front of the television where we were fed something we ultimately weren't much interested in. TV gave us few choices. Naturally, we became "couch potatoes" and many of us truly did feel like we wasted our time—as our parents so often chided us—"rotting away" in front of the TV.

I'm reading these days—ironically, on the web—that we don't read anymore. People often confess this same thing to me when they hear I'm a poet. The other day, I was opening up a bank account and the associate working at the bank, when he found out what I did, sighed and admitted that he doesn't read as much as he used to. I asked him whether he had a Facebook account, which he did, and a Twitter, which he also did. I asked him whether he sent and received e-mails. Yes, he said, many every day. I told him that he was, in fact, reading and writing a lot. We're reading and writing more than we have in a generation, but we are doing it differently—skimming, parsing, grazing, bookmarking, forwarding, and spamming language—in ways that aren't yet recognized as literary, but with a panoply of writers using the raw material of the web as the basis for their works it's only a matter of time until it is.

I keep reading that in the age of screens we've lost our ability to concentrate, that we've become distracted, unable to focus. But when I look around me and see people riveted to their devices, I've never seen such a great wealth of concentration, focus, and engagement. I find it ironic that those who say we have no concentration are most bothered by how addicted people are to their devices. I find it equally ironic that most of the places I read about how addicted we are to the web is on the web itself, scattered across numerous websites, blog posts, tweets, and Facebook pages.

On those blogs, I read how the Internet has made us antisocial, how we've lost the ability to have a conversation. But when I see people with their devices, all I see is people communicating with one another: texting, chatting, IM'ing. And I have to wonder, In what way is this not social? A conversation broken up into short bursts and quick emoticons is still a conversation. Watch someone's face while they're in the midst of a rapid-fire text message exchange: it's full of human emotion and expression—anticipation, laughter, affect. Critics claim that even having a device present acts to inhibit conversation, and that the best antidote to our technological addiction is a return to good old-fashioned face-to-face conversation. They say, "Conversation is there for us to reclaim. For the failing connections of our digital world, it is the talking cure." But this seems to ignore the fact that smartphones are indeed phones: two-way devices for human-to-human conversations, replete with expressive vocal cadence and warmth. Is conversation over the telephone still—140 years after the phone was invented—somehow not considered "intimate" enough, lessened because it is mediated by technology?

But beyond that, life is still full of attentive, engaged face-to-face conversations and close listening, be it at the many conferences, lectures, or readings I attend where large audiences hang on every word the speakers say, or my own therapy sessions—nothing more than two people in a room—the tenor and intensity of which hasn't changed in decades despite several technological revolutions. When a student comes and finds me during office hours, that student—normally tethered to their device—can still go deep without one. Even my seventeen-year-old son, awash in social media, still demands that we "talk" in the darkness of his bedroom each night before he goes to sleep, just as we have done his entire life. It's a ritual that neither of us are willing to forgo in spite of our love of gadgets. Everywhere I look—on the street, in restaurants and cafés, in classrooms, or waiting in line for a movie—in spite of dire predictions, people still seem to know how to converse.

Our devices, if anything, tend to amplify our sociability. Sometimes we converse face-to-face, other times over our devices, but often, it's a combination of the two. I'm in a hotel lobby and I'm watching two fashionable women in their twenties sitting next to each other on a modernist sofa. They are parallel with one another: their shoulders are touching; their legs are extended with their feet resting on a table in front of them. They're both cradling their devices, each in their own world. From time to time, they hold their phones up and share something on-screen before retreating into their respective zones. While they peck away at their keyboards, shards of conversation pass between them, accompanied by laughter, head nods, and pointing. Then, at once, they put their phones in their purses, straighten up their bodies, angle toward one another, and launch into a fully attentive face-to-face conversation. They're now very animated, gesticulating with their hands; you can feel the words being absorbed into their bodies, which are vehicles for augmenting what they're saying. It's fascinating: just a moment ago it was parallel play; now it's fully interactive. They continue this way for several more minutes until, as if again on cue, they both reach into their purses, take out their phones, and resume their previous postures, shoulders once again touching and legs outstretched. They're no longer conversing with each other, but are now conversing with someone unseen. Our devices might be changing us, but to say that they're dehumanizing us is simply wrong.

The Internet has been accused of making us shallow. We're skimming, not reading. We lack the ability to engage deeply with a subject anymore. That's both true and not true: we skim and browse certain types of content, and read others carefully. Oftentimes, we'll save a long form journalism article and read it later offline, perhaps on the train home from work. Accusations like those tend to assume we're all using our devices the same way. But looking over the shoulders of people absorbed in their devices on the subway, I see many people reading newspapers and books on their phones and many others playing Candy Crush Saga. Sometimes someone will be glancing at a newspaper one moment and playing a game the next. There's a slew of blogs I've seen recently which exhaustively document photos of people reading paper books on the subway. One photographer nostalgically claims that he wanted to capture a fading moment when "books are vanishing and are being replaced by characterless iPads and Kindles." But that's too simple, literally judging a book by its cover. Who's to say what they're reading? Often we assume that just because someone is reading a book on a device that it's trashy. Sometimes it is; sometimes it isn't. Last night I walked into the living room and my wife was glued to her iPad, reading the *Narrative of the Life of Frederick Douglass*. Hours later, when I headed to bed she hadn't moved an inch, still transfixed by this 171-year-old narrative on her twenty-first-century device. When I said good night, she didn't even look up.

And while these critics tell us time and again that our brains are being rewired, I'm not so sure that's all bad. Every new media requires new ways of thinking. How strange it would be if in the midst of this digital revolution we were still expected to use our brains in the same way we read books or watched TV? The resistance to the Internet shouldn't surprise us: cultural reactionaries defending the status quo have been around as long as media has. Marshall McLuhan tells us that television was written off by people invested in literature as merely "mass entertainment" just as the printed book was met with the same skepticism in the sixteenth century by scholastic philosophers. McLuhan says that "the vested interests of acquired knowledge and conventional wisdom have always been by-passed and engulfed by new media . . . The student of media soon comes to expect the new media of any period whatever to be classed as pseudo by those who have acquired the patterns of earlier media, whatever they may happen to be."

I'm told that our children are most at risk, that the excessive use of computers has led our kids to view the real world as fake. But I'm not so sure that even I can distinguish "real" from "fake" in my own life. How is my life on Facebook any less "real" than what happens in my day-to-day life? In fact, much of what does happen in my day-to-day life comes through Facebook—work opportunities, invitations to dinner parties, and even the topics I discuss at those dinner parties often comes from stuff I've found out about on Facebook. It's also likely that I met more than a few of my dinner companions via social media.

I'm reading that screen time makes kids antisocial and withdrawn, but when I see my kids in front of screens, they remind me of those women on the couch, fading in and out, as they deftly negotiate the space of the room with the space of the web. And when they're, say, gaming, they tend to get along beautifully, deeply engaged with what is happening on the screen while being highly sensitive to each other; not a move of their body or expression of emotion gets overlooked. Gaming ripples through their entire bodies: they kick their feet, jump for joy, and scream in anger. It's hard for me to see in what way this could be considered disconnected. It's when they leave the screens that trouble starts: they start fighting over food or who gets to sit where in the car. And, honestly, after a while they get bored of screens. There's nothing like a media-soaked Sunday morning to make them beg me to take them out to the park to throw a football or to go on a bike ride.

It's Friday night and my teenage son has invited about a dozen of his buddies—boys and girls—over to the house. They're sprawled out on the couch, mostly separated by gender, glued to their smartphones. Over by the TV, a few kids are playing video games that along with their yelps and whoops are providing the soundtrack for the evening. The group on the couch are close, emotionally and physically; they form a long human chain, shoulders snuggled up against their neighbor's. Some of the girls are leaning into the other girls, using them as pillows. The boys are physical with each other, but differently: they reach out occasionally to fist bump or high-five. One couple, a boyfriend and girlfriend, are clumped in the middle of the couch, draped on top of one another, while at the same time pressed up against the others.

There's an electric teenage energy to the group. They're functioning as a group, yet they're all independent. They spend long periods in silence; the only noises emanating from the gang are the occasional sounds that are emitted from their devices—pings, plonks, chimes, and tinny songs from YouTube pages. Bursts of laughter are frequent, starting with one person and spreading like wildfire to the others. As they turn their devices toward one another, I hear them saying, "Have you seen this?" and shrieking, "Oh my god!" Laughter ripples again, dying out quickly. Then they plunge back into concentrated silence. Out of the blue, one of the kids on the couch playfully says to the other, "You jerk! I can't believe you just sent me that!" And it's then that I realize that as much as they're texting and status updating elsewhere on the web, a large part of their digital communication is happening between these kids seated on the same couch.

They're constantly taking pictures of themselves and of each other. Some are shooting videos, directing their friends to make faces, to say outrageous things to the camera, or to wave hello. And then, it's right back to the devices, where those images are uploaded to social media and shared among the group, as links are blasted out—all within a minute. Suddenly, the girls shriek, "I look so ugly!" or "You look so pretty!" and "We need to take this one again." I hear someone say, "That was so funny! Let's watch it again." They count likes and favorites as they pile up and read comments that are instantly appearing from both inside and outside the room. This goes on for hours. In a sense, this is as much about creativity as it is about communication. Each photo, posed and styled, is considered with a public response in mind. They are excited by the idea of themselves as images. But why wouldn't they be? From before the moment they were born, my kids have been awash in images of themselves, beginning with the fuzzy in utero sonograms that they now have pinned to their bedroom walls. Since then, our cameras—first clumsy digital cameras and now smartphones—have been a constant presence in their life, documenting their every move. We never took just one picture of them but took dozens in rapid-fire fashion, off-loaded them to the computer, and never deleted a single one. Now, when I open my iPhoto album to show them their baby pictures, the albums look like Andy Warhol paintings, with the same images in slight variations repeated over and over, as we documented them second by second. Clearly we have created this situation.

There is no road map for this territory. They are making it up as they go along. But there's no way that this evening could be considered asocial or antisocial. Their imaginations are on full throttle and are wildly engaged in what they're doing. They are highly connected and interacting with each other, but in ways that are pretty much unrecognizable to me. I'm struggling to figure out what's so bad about this. I'm reading that screen addiction is taking a terrible toll on our children, but in their world it's not so much an addiction as a necessity. Many key aspects of our children's lives are in some way funneled through their devices. From online homework assignments to research prompts, right on down to where and when soccer practice is going to be held, the information comes to them via their devices. (And yes, my kids love their screens and love soccer.)

After reading one of these hysterical "devices are ruining your child" articles, my sister-in-law decided to take action. She imposed a system whereby, after dinner, the children were to "turn in" their devices—computers, smartphones, and tablets—to her. They could "check them out" over the course of the evening, but only if they could explain exactly what they needed them for, which had to be for "educational purposes." But if there was no reason to check them out, the devices stayed with my sister-in-law until they were given back the next day for their allotted after-school screen time, which she also monitors. Upon confiscating my nephew's cell phone one Friday night, she asked him on Saturday morning, "What plans do you have with your friends today?" "None," he responded. "You took away my phone."

On a family vacation, after a full day of outdoor activities that included seeing the Grand Canyon and hiking, my friend and her family settled into the hotel for the evening. Her twelve-year-old daughter is a fan of preteen goth girl crafting videos on YouTube, where she learns how to bedazzle black skull T-shirts and make perfectly ripped punk leggings and home-brewed perfumes. That evening, the girl selected some of her favorite videos to share with her mother. After agreeing to watch a few, her mother grew impatient. "This is nice, but I don't want to spend the whole night clicking around." The daughter indignantly responded that she wasn't just "clicking around." She was connecting with a community of girls her own age who shared similar interests. Her mother was forced to reconsider her premise that her daughter wasn't just wasting time on the Internet; instead, she was fully engaged, fostering an aesthetic, feeding her imagination, indulging in her creative proclivities, and hanging out with her friends, all from the comfort of a remote hotel room perched on the edge of the Grand Canyon.

In theorizing or discussing our time spent online, we tend to oversimplify what is an extraordinarily nuanced experience, full of complexity and contradiction. The way we speak about technology belies our monolithic thinking about it. During his recent run for president, a number of Donald Trump's legal depositions were scrutinized by the *New York Times*, which intended to show how Trump spoke when he wasn't in the spotlight. During a series of questions about the ways he used technology, he was asked about television, to which he replied, "I don't have a lot of time for listening to television." I was struck by the phrase "listening to television." You don't really listen to television; you watch it. You listen exclusively to radio. Born in 1946, it's safe to assume that Trump spent his formative years listening to radio. My father, roughly the same age as Trump, says similar things. Growing up, he used to berate us kids for watching TV, saying that it took no imagination. Waxing nostalgic, he'd say, "When I was a boy listening to radio, you had to make up everything in your mind. You kids have it all there for you." For my father—and I can imagine Trump, too—although they watched television, I don't think they really understood it. Certainly, Trump's statement belies a basic misapprehension of the medium.

Trump's comment is a textbook example of Marshall McLuhan's theory which states that the content of any medium is always another medium: "The content of writing is speech, just as the written word is the content of print, and print is the content of the telegraph." For Trump, the content of TV is radio. It's common for people to pick up everything they know about a previous medium and throw it at a newer one. I'm often reminded of Trump's comment when I hear complaints about how we're wasting time on the Internet. To them, television is the content of the web. What they seem to be missing is that the web is not monolithic, but instead is multiple, diverse, fractured, contradictory, high, and low, all at the same time in ways that television rarely was.

It's a Sunday morning and I go downstairs to get the *New York Times*. In the travel section is a piece entitled "Going Off the Grid on a Swedish Island." It's about a woman who takes a digital detox on a remote island as a reminder that she is not, in fact, "merely the sum of my posts and tweets and filter-enhanced iPhone photos." She checks herself into a "hermit hut"—an isolated cabin without electricity or running water—and gives her phone to her husband who locks it with a pass code. As she settles into the hut, bereft of her technology, she suddenly discovers herself connected to nature, listening to the sound of waves folding by the nearby shore. She also rediscovers the pleasure of reading books. She becomes introspective, remarking, "Now, disconnected from the imposed (or imagined) pressures from followers and friends loitering unseen in the ether of the Web, I found myself reaching for a more authentic, balanced existence for myself, online and off."

She takes long walks. But each natural experience she has is filtered through the lens of technology. While listening to the sounds of nature, she muses, "Without a Spotify playlist to lose myself in . . . What else had I been blind to while distracted by electronics, I wondered?" She sees marvelous things: towering wind turbines, whose "graceful blades whoosh audibly overhead," and congratulates herself when she resists the urge to record and share the scene on social media. She conveniently forgets the fact that these turbines are wholly designed and driven by digital interfaces. She nostalgically finds older, predigital technologies—ironically littering the landscape—charming. Seeing an upturned rotting car that "looks like a bug," she can't resist: "I pulled out my camera and took a photo, one that I knew would never get a single 'like' from anyone but me. And that was just fine." On these sojourns, she mechanizes nature, describing it with tech metaphors: "Along the way, the only tweets I encountered were from birds." On her final evening on the island, she has a cosmic epiphany whilst musing on the stars in the night sky, one that is served with a dose of self-flagellation for her previous misdeeds: "Those spellbinding heavens are always hiding in plain sight above us, if only we would unplug long enough to notice."

Even in such lighthearted Sunday morning fare, her words are laced with an all-too-pervasive, unquestioning guilt about technology. Try as she might, the writer is enmeshed with technology to the point that she is unable to experience nature without technological mediation. She may have left her devices at home, but she's still seeing the world entirely through them. Her brain, indeed, has become differently wired and all the nature in the world on a weekend digital detox won't change that. What was accomplished by this trip? Not much. Far away from her devices, all she did was think obsessively about them. Returning from her trip, it's hard to imagine that much changed. I can't imagine that in the spirit of her adventure she wrote her piece out longhand in number 2 pencils on legal pads by candlelight, only to sit down at a Remington typewriter bashing out the final draft, and filing it via carrier pigeon. No. Instead, the morning her piece appeared, she retweeted a link to the article: ".@ingridkwilliams goes off the grid on a charming Swedish island."

What these types of articles tend to ignore is the fact that technology has been entwined with nature for as long as humans have been depicting it. French landscape painters such as Claude Lorrain (1600–1682) often painted what they called ideal landscapes, which rendered nature in pitch-perfect states that never existed. So you get classical ruins nestled in dense, thick jungles that couldn't possibly grow in the rocky Greek soil. These painters claimed that architecture was a kind of technology, one that either represented the spoiling of nature or its conquest by man. Even Thoreau's cabin on Walden Pond was within earshot of the rattle and hum of a busy East Coast railroad line that ran about a kilometer away from his "hermit hut."

Another article in this morning's newspaper—this time in the business section—sends an identical message. It's called "Put Down the Phone." The piece focuses on various types of software and apps that monitor and restrict the time you spend on social media. These technologies include wearable clothing—with a sweep of an arm you can silence your phone—and suggests twelve-step-style parlor games you can play with your friends: the winner is the one who looks at their phone the least. There's also a review of an app that turns your smartphone back into a "dumb phone" circa 1999 that does nothing more than make and receive calls.

But the highlight of the article is a plastic facsimile of a smartphone that is a piece of plastic that does absolutely nothing. It's touted as "a security blanket for people who want to curb their phone addiction but are afraid to leave home without something to hold on to." And yet in psychoanalytic theory, a security blanket is known as a transitional object, one that represents "me" and "not me" simultaneously. That definition—me and not me simultaneously—seems to be a more realistic assessment of our online lives than the tirade of pleas for a return to some long-lost, unified "authentic" self. Online, I am me and not me at the same time. Surely, the way I portray myself on Facebook isn't really me; it's an image of myself as I wish to project it to the world. Sometimes that image is true. Other times it's a complete lie.

The article concludes with a quote from a psychology professor at the University of Kansas, who disparagingly says, "Smartphones are a potent delivery mechanism for two fundamental human impulses: our quest to find new and interesting distractions, and our desire to feel that we have checked off a task." But I find that to be positive. That quote sums up the complex balancing act we perform with our devices. We're productive—we're checking off tasks—and we're distracted in new and interesting ways. (Since when are *new* and *interesting* pejorative?) It's that frisson of opposites—bacon-infused chocolate or salted caramel ice cream—that makes it zing. The professor goes on to bemoan the fact that "with these devices you can get that sense of accomplishment multiple times a minute. The brain gets literally rewired to switch—to constantly seek out novelty, which makes putting the phone down difficult." It sounds great to me. Novelty *and* accomplishment. They work together.

When I used to watch TV, "likes" weren't really part of the game. Sure, I liked one show better than another, but I was forced to choose from a tiny set of options, seven channels, to be specific. Today, "like" has come to mean something very different. We can support something, expressing ourselves by clicking Like or we can download something we like. In this way, we build a rich ecosystem of artifacts around us based on our proclivities and desires. What sits in my download folder—piles of books to be read, dozens of movies to be watched, and hundreds of albums to be heard—constitutes a sort of self-portrait of both who I am in this particular point in time, and who I was in earlier parts of my life. In fact, you'll find nestled among the Truffaut films several episodes of *The Brady Bunch*, a show I really "liked" back in the day. Sometimes I'm in the mood to watch Truffaut; other times I'm in the mood to watch *The Brady Bunch*. Somehow those impulses don't contradict one another; instead, they illuminate the complexities of being me. I'm rarely just one way: I like high art sometimes and crap others.

While I could discuss any number of musical epiphanies I've personally experienced over the past half century, all of them would pale in comparison to the epiphany of seeing Napster for the first time in 1999. Although prior to Napster I had been a member of several file-sharing communities, the sheer scope, variety, and seeming endlessness of Napster was mind-boggling: you never knew what you were going to find and how much of it was going to be there. It was as if every record store, flea market, and thrift shop in the world had been connected by a searchable database and flung their doors open, begging you to walk away with as much as you could carry for free. But it was even better because the supply never exhausted; the coolest record you've ever dug up could now be shared with all your friends. Of course this has been exacerbated many times over with the advent of torrents and MP3 blogs.

But the most eye-opening thing about Napster was the idea that you could browse other people's shared files. It was as if a little private corner of everyone's world was now publicly available for all to see. It was fascinating—perhaps even a bit voyeuristic—to see what music other people had in their folders and how they organized it. One of the first things that struck me about Napster was how impure and eclectic people's tastes were. Whilst browsing another user's files, I was stunned to find John Cage MP3s alphabetically snuggled up next to, say, Mariah Carey files in the same directory. It boggled the mind: how could a fan of thorny avant-garde music also like the sugary pop of Mariah Carey? And yet it's true. Everyone has guilty pleasures. But never before have they been so exposed—and celebrated—this publicly. To me, this was a great relief. It showed that online—and by extension in real life—we never have been just one way, all the time. That's too simple. Instead, we're a complex mix, full of contradictions.

The web is what Stanford professor Sianne Ngai calls "*stuplime*," a combination of the stupid and the sublime. That cat video on BuzzFeed is so stupid, but its delivery mechanism—Facebook—is so mind-bogglingly sublime. Inversely, that dashboard cam of the meteor striking Russia is so cosmically sublime, but its delivery mechanism—Facebook—is so mind-bogglingly stupid. It's this tension that keeps us glued to the web. Were it entirely stupid or were it entirely sublime, we would've gotten bored long ago. A befuddling mix of logic and nonsense, the web by its nature is surrealist: a shattered, contradictory, and fragmented medium. What if, instead of furiously trying to stitch together these various shards into something unified and coherent—something many have been desperately trying to do—we explore the opposite: embracing the disjunctive as a more organic way of framing what is, in essence, a medium that defies singularity?

Shattered by technology, modernism embraced the jagged twentieth-century media landscape and the fragmentation it brought, claiming it to be emblematic of its time. Not to overstretch the analogy—it's a new century with new technologies—but there are bits and pieces salvageable from the smoldering wreckage of modernism from which we might extract clues on how to proceed in the digital age. In retrospect, the modernist experiment was akin to a number of planes barreling down runways—cubist planes, surrealist planes, abstract expressionist planes, and so forth—each taking off, and then crashing immediately, only to be followed by another aborted takeoff, one after another. What if, instead, we imagine that these planes didn't crash at all, but sailed into the twenty-first century, and found full flight in the digital age? What if the cubist airplane gave us the tools to theorize the shattered surfaces of our interfaces or the surrealist airplane gave us the framework through which to theorize our distraction and waking dream states or the abstract expressionist airplane provided us with a metaphor for our all-over, skein-like networks? Our twenty-first-century aesthetics are fueled by the blazing speed of the networks, just as futurist poems a century ago were founded on the pounding of industry and the sirens of war.

Literary modernism provides insights as well. Could we theorize our furious file sharing through Freud's ideas about the archive, our ROM and RAM through his perception-consciousness system? Could we imagine the web as the actualization of Jorge Luis Borges's infinite library of Babel, as described in his famous 1941 short story of the same name? Could we envision Twitter's 140-character constraint as being a direct descendent of Hemingway's brilliant one-line novel: "For sale: baby shoes, never worn." Are Joseph Cornell's boxes palm-sized, handheld pre-Internet devices, replete with icons and navigational systems? Is *Finnegans Wake* a wellspring of hashtags? Postmodernism's sampling and remixing—so predominant in mainstream culture from karaoke to gaming to hip-hop—are also foundational to the mechanics of the web. If the Internet is one big replication device, then every artifact flowing through it is subject to its bouncy reverberatory gestures (the retweet, for example), a situation where an artifact's primary characteristic, to quote Roland Barthes, is "a tissue of quotations drawn from the innumerable centers of culture," while at the same time remaining a container of content.

When futurist poet F. T. Marinetti famously wrote in a 1909 manifesto that "we will destroy the museums, libraries, academies of every kind," he could not have foreseen the double-edged sword of web-based structures. On one hand, artists are embracing the meme's infinitesimal life span as a new metric (think: short attention span as a new avant-garde), constructing works not for eternity but only for long enough to ripple across the networks, vanishing as quickly as they appear, replaced by new ones tomorrow. On the other hand, our every gesture is archived by search engines and cemented into eternally recallable databases. Unlike Marinetti's call to erase history, on the web everything is forever. The Internet itself is a giant museum, library, and academy all in one, comprised of everything from wispy status updates to repositories of dense classical texts. And every moment you spend wasting time on the Internet contributes to the pile—even your clicks, favorites, and likes. Read through a literary lens, could we think of our web sojourns as epic tales effortlessly and unconsciously written, etched into our browser histories as a sort of new memoir? Beyond that, in all its glory and hideousness, Facebook is the greatest collective autobiography that a culture has ever produced, a boon to future sociologists, historians, and artists.

This accretion of data is turning us into curators, librarians, and amateur archivists, custodians of our own vast collections. The web's complex ecosystem of economies—both paid and pirated—offer us more cultural artifacts than we can consume: There are more movies on Netflix than I will ever be able to see, not to mention all the movies I've simultaneously downloaded from file-sharing which languish unwatched on my hard drive. The fruits of what's known as "free culture"—the idea that the web should be a place for an open exchange of ideas and intellectual materials, bereft of over-restrictive copyright laws—create a double-edged sword. Abundance is a lovely problem to have, but it produces a condition whereby the management of my cultural artifacts—their acquisition, filing, redundancy, archiving, and redistribution—is overwhelming their actual content. I tend to shift my artifacts around more than I tend to use them. And all of those artifacts—jaggy AVIs, fuzzy PDFs, lossy MP3s—are decidedly lo-res. I've happily swapped quality for quantity, uniqueness for reproduction, strength for weakness, and high resolution for super compression in order to participate in the global cornucopia of file sharing and social media. And what of consumption? I've outsourced much of it. While I might only be able to read a fraction of what I've downloaded, web spiders—indexing automatons— have read it all. While part of me laments this, another part is thrilled at the rare opportunity to live in one's own time, able to reimagine the status of the cultural object in the twenty-first century where context is the new content.

The web ecology runs on quantity. Quantity is what

drove the vast data leaks of Julian Assange, Aaron Swartz, Chelsea Manning, and Edward Snowden, leaks so absurdly large they could never be read in their entirety, only parsed, leaks so frighteningly huge they were derided by the mainstream media as "information vandalism," a critique that mistook the leak's form for function—or malfunction—as if to say the gesture of liberating information is as important as what's actually being moved. To Assange, Swartz, Manning, and Snowden, what was being moved *was* important—a matter of life and death. But then again to many of us, our devices are a matter of life and death. The ubiquity of smartphones and dashboard and body cams, combined with the ability to distribute these images virally, have shed light on injustices that previously went unnoticed. When critics insist we put down our devices because they are making us less connected to one another, I have to wonder how the families of Tamir Rice or Laquan McDonald might react to that.

This book attempts to reconcile these contradictions and embrace these multiplicities as a means of reenriching, reenlivening, recuperating, and reclaiming the time we spend in front of screens—time that is almost always dismissed as being wasted. Scrawled across the walls of Paris in May 1968, the slogan "live without dead time" became a rallying cry for a way of reclaiming spaces and bureaucracies that suck the life from you. I'd like to think our web experience can be nearly bereft of dead time if only we had the lens through which to see it that way. I don't mean to paint too rosy a picture. The downsides of the web are well known: trolling, hate, flame wars, spam, and rampant stupidity. Still, there's something perverse about how well we use the web yet how poorly we theorize our time spent on it. I'm hearing a lot of complaints, but I'm not getting too many answers, which makes me think perhaps our one-dimensional approach has been wrongheaded. Befitting a complex medium, one that is resistant to singularities, let's consider a panoply of ideas, methods, and inspirations. The word "rhizomatic" has been used to describe the web to the point of cliché, but I still find it useful. The rhizome, a root form that grows unpredictably in all directions, offers many paths rather than one. The genie will not be put back in the bottle. Walking away is not an option. We are not unplugging anytime soon. Digital detoxes last as long as grapefruit diets do; transitional objects are just that. I'm convinced that learning, interaction, conversation, and engagement continues as it always has, but it's taking new and different forms. I think it's time to drop the simplistic guilt about wasting time on the Internet and instead begin to explore—and perhaps even celebrate—the complex possibilities that lay before us.

CHAPTER 1

The Social Network

One crisp Saturday morning in the fall of 2014, I announced a new course on my modest Twitter feed: "My class, called Wasting Time on the Internet, will be offered @Penn next semester," along with a link to the course description:

> *We spend our lives in front of screens, mostly wasting time: checking social media, watching cat videos, chatting, and shopping. What if these activities—clicking, SMSing, status updating, and random surfing—were used as raw material for creating compelling and emotional works of literature? Could we reconstruct our autobiography using only Facebook? Could we write a great novella by plundering our Twitter feed? Could we reframe the Internet as the greatest poem ever written? Using our laptops and a Wi-Fi connection as our only materials, this class will focus on the alchemical recuperation of aimless surfing into substantial works of literature. Students will be required to stare at the screen for three hours, only interacting through*

chat rooms, bots, social media, and LISTSERVs. To bolster our practice, we'll explore the long history of the recuperation of boredom and time wasting through critical texts. Distraction, multitasking, and aimless drifting is mandatory.

A few hours later, when I checked back, the tweet had gone viral, accompanied by comments like: "Wait I believe I already have a PhD in that" and "I'd ace it." In my feed was a request from *Vice* for an interview, which I gave a day later. Shortly afterward, I found a message in my inbox from the *Washington Post* also requesting an interview, which I gave. From then on, I was inundated daily with interview requests, all of which—with the exception of some mainstream television shows—I declined. With a shortage of new chum in the waters from me, what ensued was a media feeding frenzy, which ultimately ended up consuming itself.

After the two interviews in *Vice* and the *Washington Post*, I noticed a spate of second-tier news sites that basically reprinted the *Vice* and *Post* pieces in their entirety, slapped on new opening and concluding sentences, gave it a new title, and added a byline. A few days later, a bunch of third-tier sites did the same thing to the text of the second-tier sites. It was a massive game of copy and paste, far from what we consider to be upholding standards of original journalism. It was an object lesson not only on how information travels in a world of cut and paste but also how quickly it can devolve into distorted disinformation.

With the torrents of press—good and bad—the waiting list for the class had swelled to more than one hundred students for only fifteen seats. After much anticipation, the class finally convened in January 2015 in an oak-paneled Ivy League room. The surroundings—which included a huge oval antique wooden table around which the class gathered—were incongruous with the task at hand. Yet this distinguished room was equipped with racks of audio, video, and Internet equipment, as well as a flat-screen monitor that adorned an otherwise empty wall above the classical wainscoting. An antique chandelier hovered over the table. Because of its location on the university backbone of the Internet, the Wi-Fi in the room was industrial strength. The students filtered into the room, opened their laptops, and—without a word—began wasting time on the Internet. Few instructions were given other than the fact that "something" needed to be written and submitted, culled from these sessions.

From the start, it was a disaster. The students drifted aimlessly for three hours barely using the social media and LISTSERVs that had been set up for them. With no one to guide or critique them, the writing they produced at the end of each session was dreadful, reflecting the unfocused experience they were having in this class. During cigarette breaks, the students looked isolated, exhausted, and irritated. I wasn't sure what to do. In my decade of teaching at Penn, I had never seen a group of students as demoralized as these. Clearly, my experiment was failing.

After one of those breaks, I was sitting at a table outside the room trying to figure out how to solve this mess with my TA when, from out of nowhere, music started blasting from behind the closed doors in the classroom. When we got up to see what was going on, we found all fifteen students, up out of their chairs, dancing madly to Khia's X-rated rap song "My Neck, My Back," which was blaring from all fifteen laptops streaming the identical YouTube video. One student commandeered the huge screen on the wall by jacking his computer into it, playing the video on the monitor, and pumping the sound through the room's speakers. The room resembled a cross between a television showroom—where all the TVs are lined up in a row playing the same show— and a disco. I wasn't sure what happened, but something had changed.

As it turns out, one of the students sent a request to the LISTSERV in silence, asking everyone to participate in a writing exercise she needed help with. Her idea was for everyone in the room to pick a song and play it aloud. She would then listen to the cacophony of lyrics and write down snippets from random lyrics she heard, coming up with an audio portrait in words. The students obliged, but the cacophony of fifteen computers each playing a different song proved to be too overwhelming for her to extract anything worthwhile. Instead, breaking the rules, the class began a lively discussion, brainstorming on how they could help make her project better. They decided to see what would happen if they all played the same song at the same time, which was, in short, how they stopped writing and started dancing. As soon as that song ended, they began debating the next song to play. The video was queued, and on the count of three, everyone pushed Start. The next song began, and the dancing resumed. For the next two hours, until the class ended, all they did was dance.

The next week in class, fully energized and working as a group, they began to throw around other ideas for wasting time on the Internet that they could do together. Gone was the lethargy; gone was the silence. In their place, dozens of ideas flew around the room, which were debated and tested. Some were great; many failed.

One particularly provocative idea was for everybody to open their laptops and pass them to the person seated to their left. For the next minute, that person could open anything on the laptop—any document, folder, or file. The only rules were that nothing could be altered or deleted and, for transparency's sake, no windows that had been opened could be closed. At the end of a minute, the laptops would be passed again to the person sitting to the left of them, and so forth, until every machine had traveled around the table and fifteen different people had a turn with everybody's computer. Upon hearing this proposition, my students' faces went white. I could feel the fear rippling through the room. There was hesitation. Some expressed reservations: "My whole life is on that laptop!" or "I've never allowed anyone to touch my laptop before." But once they realized that everyone was in the same position of radical vulnerability, they agreed to cautiously proceed.

What transpired was both fascinating and a bit anticlimactic. I saw one woman hesitantly eyeing someone's laptop, which had landed in front of her. She pecked at a few keys, opened a couple of windows, and passed it on. I watched another student as he dug a few levels deep into a directory, found a Word document, opened it, glanced quickly at it, and proceeded to dig around some more. Finally, when your laptop made its way back to you, you saw exactly what everyone had looked at. My laptop returned with my iPhoto open, several of my downloaded videos playing, and a bunch of financial spreadsheets cracked. Someone had gone through my e-mails; someone searched for the word "porn"; someone else took a peek at my book in progress. Upon inspecting their computers, they had a variety of responses, mostly of amusement. As it turns out, even if, for example, somebody's diaries were found, there hadn't been enough time to uncover the juicy parts. After all, there wasn't much to see in a minute's time, and revenge awaited: they'd have a turn with your laptop soon enough.

The exercise was demystifying. It began to dawn on everybody that what we have on our laptops is, by and large, the same as what everyone else has on their laptops—a jumble of documents and files that mean a lot to us—but unless someone was looking for something very specific, our stuff didn't matter much to anybody else. Afterward, I could feel a palpable sense of relief in the room. I could see my students' bodies relaxing and the tension draining from their faces as they began connecting with their neighbors, sharing what other people opened, and laughing about it. What they feared—a massive invasion of privacy—didn't happen in the ways they feared it would. Instead, the opposite happened: the room felt deeply connected, physically and emotionally, through those interactions with machines. They took a risk and as a result found themselves having crossed a certain threshold, one that allowed new levels of trust and intimacy and permitted them to move forward as a group into uncharted waters.

The stakes got higher: they began doing "data duels," in which two people would get up in front of the class, exchange laptops, stand back-to-back, walk ten paces, turn around, face each other, and, at the count of three, each would delete one document from the other's computer and empty the trash. Before handing the laptops back, all windows were closed so they'd never know which document was deleted. A year later, I still have no idea which documents I lost, which reminds me that maybe my data isn't as precious as I thought it was.

Over the months, the class evolved into an idea generator on how a group of people in a room could waste time on the Internet together:

> *Venmo $100 to the person to your right. They must then Venmo $100 to the person to their right and so on until your money goes full circle and returns to you.*
>
> *Work in a group to invent a rumor. Spread the rumor on as many social media sites as possible.*
>
> *Do a background check on the person to your left. Find*

every detail about them: addresses, schools, e-mail, hobbies, groups, publications, work, criminal record, family members, etc. Find everything you can by any means necessary. Hack into their accounts if necessary. Save what you find in a document. Send it to them.

In a group, have everyone put their addresses in a bowl in the middle and each person draws one at random. Go to eBay and buy that person a present for less than one dollar.

As a group, choose a popular album of music. Find the worst possible versions of each song on the web, be it a terrible cover on YouTube, a bad-quality download, a virus-laden download, a misheard lyrics version, or a horrible remix. Reconstruct the album out of these new versions.

One week, a challenge was made to see who, after fifteen minutes, could tally the largest dollar amount by adding things to their Amazon shopping cart. When it was finished, the winner tallied $23,475,104.18 by clicking on vintage postage stamps, sports memorabilia, and expensive jewelry. Most people quickly emptied everything in their cart, fearing that they'd mistakenly hit a Buy button, putting them into debt for thousands or even millions of dollars. I forgot to empty mine, whereupon the next day at work, I got a panicked call from my wife, freaked out that someone had hacked our Amazon account to the tune of $2.5 million. I had some explaining to do. After each exercise, everyone in the room would restart their computer—a ceremonial cleansing that became a ritual. As computer start-up chimes tolled throughout the room, it was a sign that it was time to begin a new activity.

And so it went, week after week. I soon dropped the writing requirement, for the experience of wasting time on the Internet together in the same room far surpassed any artifact that would result from it. We came to the conclusion that when we waste time on the Internet, we usually do it alone or as a parallel activity—like in a dorm or a library—which is why the first few classes failed. By inserting the network and machine into the midst of physically based social interaction, new forms of communal activity were possible. The class was remarkably close to the experience of playing Twister, in which physical commands are decreed by an apparatus—the spinner—which tells you where to put your hands and feet. Because you must follow the edicts of the machine (the spinner is a primitive machine) your body ends up in places it normally wouldn't. Even when those positions are awkward—your nose ends up in somebody's crotch—no offense is taken because it's the machine that dictates where the body goes. Arguably, that's what makes it fun. (It's been said that Twister was the first board game to ever use human beings as pieces.) We all agreed to play together and play by the rules, whatever the outcome may be. The presence of machines at the center of our social interactions seemed to temper whatever emotional responses we had to what were, at times, some white-knuckle moments. Like Twister, if things got too uncomfortable, we could always blame it on the machine rather than on a fellow student. Emotionally, the tone stayed cool, often verging on flat and mechanical, even when they were having fun. The dancing was wild, but wholly self-conscious; after all, this was an Ivy League university not a nightclub. There was no catharsis; we never had a group hug. Instead, there was a lot of affect flying around the room.

Affect is the powerful but often invisible emotional temperature in any given social situation, for instance, when you walk into a room that feels so tense you could "cut it with a knife," although there are no visible signs of that tension. It's similar to being afraid and noticing your palms are sweating, a palpable reaction that—with the exception of a handshake—is mostly invisible to others. Sweaty palms are an affective pre-emotion, as opposed to the full-blown emotions of screaming, laughing, or crying. Perhaps the most famous instance of affect is Pavlov's dog salivating. Affect is an inventory of shimmers, nuances, and states. Contagious, leaping from one body to another, affect infects those nearby with microemotions and microfeelings, pulsating extensions of our bodies' nervous systems. Our online lives are saturated with affect, our sensations amplified and projected by the network. Our Wi-Fi networks—carriers of affect—are invisible but ubiquitous, transmitting pulses and sensations through the air that have the potential to convert to emotions when displayed on our screens. This goes a long way to explain how hyperemotional social networking is, even on such a cold platform. Affect accounts for why things go viral on the networks. An invisible force, affect makes everything contagious.

When I e-mail a resume to apply for a job, my affectual state flickers somewhere between nervousness and hope. When I receive a response from that query, my affect is anticipation that will undoubtedly convert to emotion once I open the mail. Because of the time lag—an interval of even microseconds—online communications are affective in every way; most likely the receiver of that e-mail is also in an affective state. Watching someone await a response to a text message is a demonstration of anticipatory affect in that interval. In this way, the web is telepathic: we send an e-mail, post a status update, send a Facebook message, and then we wait, anticipating the nature of the response. Web communication is like fishing; dropping a line in the water and hoping that something will bite. But because we are addressing the entire world—an unprecedented situation—we don't really know to whom we are speaking, which sometimes results in tragic misunderstanding and miscommunication: we thought we were doing one thing but it turns out we were doing something else. Still, it is telepathy that makes the vast connections possible—between writers and readers, coders and viewers, followers and friends, not to mention members of online communities—all of which is transmitted by affect.

The content of Wi-Fi is radio, an earlier affectual wireless transmission technology. Ezra Pound, writing in 1934, famously called the artist "the antennae of the race." Pound used a new technological metaphor—the radio antenna—in order to propose a visionary occult use for it. As few artists were exclusively using radio as their medium, Pound was using new technology to describe very old media: sculpture, painting, and poetry. In this way, Pound was referring to what has become known as "hauntology," a term invented by Jacques Derrida to describe "the figure of the ghost as that which is neither present, nor absent, neither dead nor alive," which also describes the way newer media is haunted by the old. In the nineteenth century, séances used machines such as the Ouija board through which voices and ideas, many of them long dead, were transmitted to the living—literally as "ghosts in the machine"; our twenty-first-century Wi-Fi transmissions bear eerie similarities.

Like the occult, affect works against narrative: it isn't conclusive or curative; instead, it's static, continual, hovering, and conditional. As a result, my class had no denouement or dramatic conclusion. In a room full of machines and gadgets it was, ironically, the body and its small human gestures— the affective gestures—that drove the class. People say that technology creates distance between people, but we found it to be just the opposite: our physical and emotive experiences were intensified through our devices. By merging our bodies with the network, we became highly attuned and acutely sensitive to everyone in the room. The class's success was predicated on our bodies being together in the same space. Telecommuting or a MOOC (massive online open course) would simply have reified typically distanced ways of being online; our experience was, to put it mildly, rather atypical. In that room, every action was a transmission. Something as simple as students turning their laptops around to share with the class what they discovered while wasting time on the Internet triggered a series of electric responses, ones that pierced every body and mind in the room. It was, literally, a meatspace social network.

I'm in a large room in Berlin—where I've been brought to lead a four-hour workshop—on a gray, rainy Saturday afternoon wasting time on the Internet with a hundred people. They've all been required to bring their laptops and devices, which are connected to a lightning-speed Wi-Fi connection. I start by telling the group a story about how I once had a student who did a project in which he took his bank PIN code, blew it up huge on a flag, and ran it up a flagpole in the center of campus in the middle of the night when no one was looking. The next day, his PIN—his most private information—was there for all to see. Of course, nobody knew the meaning of this strange string of numbers, and even if someone could figure out that it was a PIN, they'd have no idea to which account it was attached. Within a few hours, the flag was removed. His finances were untouched.

Extending the laptop data-invasion exercise I did with my class, I proposed the following: might we be able to go a step further and share our passwords with one another? I ask if anyone wants to share their password with the group. My request is met with dead silence. I can see I'm not going to get too far with this one. So instead, I demonstrate the way I construct my passwords. I crack open a Word document and make the font really big, which is projected on a screen behind me. I explain to one hundred total strangers the formula I use to create my passwords. I show them how every password I make begins with the names of the site beginning with a capital letter—Yahoo, for instance—which is then followed by a scientist's first and last name, trailed by the last four digits of one of my old landline numbers, ending with two exclamation points. So, a typical password of mine would be YahooStephenHawking6830!! or AmazonMaxPlanck2448!! The elements I chose are indicative of who I am, including my nerdy fascination for science and nostalgia for the many phone numbers I've had throughout my life, each one evoking a flood of memories every time I type them.

I ask anyone else if they would like to come up in front of the workshop and demonstrate how they make their passwords. A woman volunteers, showing us her technique, which always includes the number 410. When asked why, she said that when she was a child growing up in Denmark, 4:10 was the time her favorite television show aired. Suddenly, the room lights up with conversation. It turns out that this particular show was aired all over Europe at that identical time and many of these international participants have deep connections to this show as well. The animated memories and chatter go on for quite a while before another gentleman steps up and proceeds to walk us through his passwords. It's very confusing and no one in the room can understand it at all, which is his intention. As he explains it to us, he is a trained cryptographer, a lover of puzzles. His passwords are completely logical, but it's a different type of logic. What's beginning to emerge among the participants is that passwords are much more than something we use to get into locked rooms: they are tiny self-portraits constructed with fragments of autobiographical data that unwittingly convey who we are and how we think. Even those generic security questions you get asked are steeped in awkwardly intimate autobiography: "What is the first name of the person you first kissed?" or "What is the last name of the teacher who gave you your first failing grade?"

Next, taking a page from my Penn class, I ask everyone to cue up one song on YouTube, then full-screen it. At the same moment, everyone hits Play. The room fills up with a cacophony of one hundred different songs played from tinny speakers. Afterward, people get up to speak about what song they chose, why they chose it, and by doing so, what sort of message they were trying to project about themselves to the others. As it turns out, everyone has a reason for choosing the song they did. One man played a rap video from Tyler the Creator that his sixteen-year-old son had showed him that morning over breakfast; another woman played a current earworm, one she claimed to be her soundtrack for the summer, already laden with memories on this early mid-June day; an older gentleman played an alternative British national anthem, one he said expressed his strong political sentiments.

One song rises above the din. It's Taylor Swift's "Shake It Off," the one song everyone in the room seems to know, and because of its iconic pop hooks the one song ringing in everyone's ears long after all the other videos have been turned off. I have everyone cue up the same YouTube video of "Shake It Off." Again, at the count of three, everyone hits Play at the identical instant. One hundred laptops are displaying the first moment of the video, a row of ballet dancers at a barre doing stretches to the heavy drumbeat that begins the song. The row of dancers in the video extends to infinity across this large room like an endless Rockettes kick line. On a hundred screens, a hundred Taylor Swifts emerge from the clusters of dancers, turn toward the camera, and sing, "I stay up too late, got nothing in my brain, that's what people say." But then a lovely computer glitch happens. Due to the various laptop processing speeds and the way they connect differently to the Internet, the videos begin to play off-kilter, with some laptops ten seconds ahead and others ten seconds behind. The room becomes a large echo chamber and as the four-minute video unfurls, the asynchronization becomes more and more pronounced. The pop song is starting to sound like one of Steve Reich's early tape-loop pieces, in which two reel-to-reel recorders play an identical tape loop simultaneously. As they play, they gradually fall out of sync with one another due to microscopic differences in the machines' playback speeds, resulting in psychedelic echoes and overlays, which is what's happened to poor Taylor Swift. Gradually, the room grows quieter as each video winds down at a different speed, then ends. Finally, the slowest laptop in the room finishes—a solo performance that mimics the final shot of the video, with Taylor Swift dropping to the ground among a troupe of perfectly poised ballerinas. It's simply poetic.

Next, I have everyone open their laptops and log on to Facebook, then walk away from their computers. For the next fifteen minutes, anyone can approach any laptop and enter whatever they like in the status update windows. There's great trepidation as the participants gingerly eyeball the laptops. I see them think for a moment, then timidly type something in the window and move on to another computer. But within a few minutes, they're fully engaged, banging words into other people's lives. Some enter benign comments: "Have a nice day!" Others are more self-reflective: "You know this is not me." "I am wasting time on the Internet." "Kenneth Goldsmith made me do this." Others yet are laden with moral sentiment: "This feels so wrong to be typing into someone else's Facebook page." Several people type surrealistic sentences, nonsensical words, and spontaneous poems in the boxes. Like graffiti taggers, a few participants enter the identical cryptic phrase into each and every computer, marking their territory. When it's over, I ask several people to read what other people wrote. The room is tense. Some people smile knowingly when they hear their words read aloud; others are horrified as they read what's been scrawled on their walls. The room becomes an emotive echo chamber, with feelings zooming around the room, bouncing off Facebook pages, and back into the room again. The affect also extends outside of the room: sure enough, phones start buzzing with friends and family contacting the participants to ask if everything is alright, and if they know their Facebook accounts have been hacked. Everyone has a lot of explaining to do.

Next I ask for volunteers to come to the front of the room and waste time on the Internet publicly for all to see on the computer, which is projected on a large screen behind them. A young man approaches, his hands trembling as he logs on to Facebook. His cursor jitters, a digital manifestation of his physical condition. He hesitates, then checks his e-mail, looks at his work schedule, and deletes a wad of spam. He scrolls through Facebook, zooming past many items, slowing down to play each and every video for a split second. His web activity is an extension of his mind: we can almost see what he is thinking when he zooms past certain items on his feed or when he lingers on others.

He's been silent the entire time, but increasingly looks out at us to gauge our reaction. The more he looks at us, the more self-conscious of his actions we feel him become. He goes to YouTube and searches through a comedy feed he subscribes to and clicks on a long video by the Canadian comedian Russell Peters, which he expands to full screen. Leaning back in his chair, he folds his arms and watches the video along with us. We titter; he smiles. The video is mildly funny and sort of entertaining; he's just letting it roll. It's going on for a little too long. I can feel the affect in the form of impatience rising in our room; after all, we were here to watch him waste time on the Internet—to see how he, specifically, wastes time—but now we're stuck watching an interminable mediocre video. While he is indeed wasting time on the Internet, he's not playing along to some set of invisible rules the group seems to have invented on the spot. People begin grumbling. Finally, affect converts to full-blown emotion when a woman in the audience challenges him: "You're not wasting time on the Internet! You're just trying to entertain us. We came here to watch the way you waste time!" The young man appears to feel her words deeply. He bows his head and apologizes: "This is pretty nerve wracking. I'm sorry but I thought you'd be bored if I wasted time on the Internet the way I normally do. I feel guilty that I wasn't being entertaining enough, so I thought you'd enjoy this video." Defeated, he heads back to his seat.

A nerdy hipster dude in black thick-rimmed glasses struts up to the podium. He sits down with confidence—perhaps even with a bit of smugness—cracks a browser and goes to a password-protected academic site where he downloads an essay by Heidegger. Next he opens Spotify, where he starts streaming some atonal string quartets by Schoenberg. You can feel the eyes beginning to roll in the room. Could this guy be more pretentious? He goes further by streaming a clip of a Godard interview with the sound turned off, at which point people start begging him to sit down. He's been caught in his performance, which, while it might not have been exactly how he wastes time on the Internet—doesn't he check his Facebook like the rest of us?—belies some grain of truth. He knew his stuff and probably chose to perform a certain curated aspect of his personality. In its own way, what he did was take the opportunity to create a performance by curating a set of cultural artifacts that spoke perhaps of who he was, who he wasn't, or who he wanted us to think he was. Chances are it was a combination of all three.

The final time waster is a graduate student who begins admitting her nervousness by stating: "My pulse is jumping." She settles in and logs on to Facebook. Scrolling through her feed, she pauses and says, "I feel guilty, like I'm exposing my friends on Facebook by doing this in front of one hundred strangers." I make a mental note about how much guilt is inscribed in these exercises. She then cracks another tab, checks her Yahoo e-mail, and begins streaming Mumford and Sons' "Little Lion Man" (radio edit) on Pandora, which resembles a soundtrack for a spaghetti Western and gives her performance a cinematic quality; we now feel like we're watching a movie. Her browsing style is restless and jumpy. Quickly, she is back on Facebook, where she fullscreens a clip from Ellen DeGeneres for a brief moment, then closes it. By now, she's losing her self-consciousness and her surfing becomes rhythmic: first she checks her e-mail, then Facebook, then back to YouTube, over and over. Both structured and restless, this cycle continually repeats with slight variations over the next ten minutes. Her ease and lack of self-consciousness is infectious: I can see the other participants' body postures change; some have stretched out on the carpeted floor as they watch, their faces open and re-laxed. Her online habits have a regularity, which remind me of breathing—drawing breath in, holding it, and expelling it in regular intervals—as she rhythmically circulates from one site to another. As she has gotten into her groove, her time wasting has become organic; everyone's become nearly silent. We're in a trance. This banal room, housed in the bowels of a brutalist concrete room in Berlin has now been transformed into something resembling a yoga studio, with one hundred strangers harmoniously enraptured, swaying together in a state of buzzing electronic tranquility.

CHAPTER 2

The Walking Dead

A few weeks after returning from Berlin, I'm walking down Park Avenue on a beautiful midsummer evening. Armies of people are streaming out of their offices, most with their smartphones in hand. I am reminded of US Supreme Court Chief Justice John G. Roberts Jr.'s comment on the central role our devices play in the contemporary world: "They are such a pervasive and insistent part of daily life that the proverbial visitor from Mars might conclude they were an important feature of human anatomy." Part human, part machine, these masses peck away at their smartphones, deftly navigating the packed sidewalk the way colonies of bats traverse the night sky.

Gazing out on this technology-soaked urban landscape, I am also reminded of how fond the surrealists were of sleeping in public. Inspired by Freud, they wanted to bring dreams out of the bedroom and onto the streets. While most of us deem sleep to be a necessary remedy, a state of repair and restoration, the surrealists felt that having to be awake was an unwelcome interruption to sleep. Their greatest wish was to exist in a continual dream state. "I believe in the future resolution of these two states, dream and reality," wrote André Breton, "which are seemingly so contradictory, into a kind of absolute reality, a surreality."

In his never-ending search to join these two disparate states, Breton started attending séances, which became required attendance for all aspiring surrealists. During the séances, Breton noticed several of his acolytes nodding off. One in particular, the poet René Crevel, revealed himself as a sleep talker, babbling nonsense in the twilight of consciousness. In Crevel's dozing, Breton discovered a sort of portable séance, one that could be whisked out of the tomblike silence of the parlor and dropped into noisy public spaces, inserting the dreamer into the midst of the crowd. From then on, he convinced Crevel to start falling asleep in cafés where, once he was presumed to be fast asleep—there was always some doubt that this was just theater—he was peppered with questions by a circle of awake poets, who transcribed these conversations as the basis for future poems. Breton was delighted with the results: Crevel's answers were perfectly surreal; his responses never quite matched up with the questions, which he took as direct manifestations culled from the subconscious, a balancing act between wakefulness and sleep.

Rivalries grew among the surrealist poets as to who could be the best public sleeper. Commenting on this, Breton wrote: "Every day they want to spend more time sleeping. Their words, recorded, intoxicate them. Everywhere, anywhere, they fall asleep . . . In the cafés, and amid the beer-glasses, the saucers." One aspiring sleeper posted a note on his door each night before going to bed that read: THE POET IS WORKING.

Proposing sleepwalking as an optimal widespread societal condition, Breton once asked, "When will we have sleeping logicians, sleeping philosophers?" It seems the surrealist vision of a dream culture has been fully realized in today's technologies. We are awash in a new electronic collective unconscious; strapped to several devices, we're half-awake, half-asleep. We speak on the phone while surfing the web, partially hearing what's being said to us while simultaneously answering e-mails and checking status updates. I can't help notice that we've become very good at being distracted. Breton would be delighted.

After a long day's work, I decide to go for a run. I throw on some shorts and sneakers, strap on some headphones, grab my iPhone, and I'm out the door. When I run I generally don't set out with a plan. Instead, I let the city take me: the traffic flows and crowds of Manhattan determine where I go. Getting going is always tough at first, but about ten minutes into it, I feel a breakthrough. Some seventies dub— King Tubby, streaming over Spotify—is rolling through my headphones, and I'm starting to get my groove.

As I start to feel the rhythm of the music and the rhythm of the run, good thoughts about the structure of a book I'm working on start to emerge. Wanting to catch them during my run, I take my iPhone out of my pocket, open up the Notes app, click on Siri's voice recognition, and begin to dictate. My speech is sent over the cell network to a server, where it's shot back to my phone in the form of text. To most people passing by on the street, I look like any other jerk multitasking. They grimace at me and shake their heads as if to say, "Why can't you just run? Must you always be tethered to that device, gossiping?" Little do they know that I am actually writing a book.

I'm in a semiconscious state: my feet are moving and my body is sweating. The thoughts are really flowing now, so much so that I almost forget I'm running as I float effortlessly above the pavement on a runner's high. In addition to the rhythms of the city, my run is determined by my interactions with technology. Every time I click voice recognition, King Tubby is paused. I change the way I speak to accommodate Siri. I want her to be able to recognize everything I'm saying, so I slow down my speech and tend to overpronounce words. I say the word "comma" every time I want to insert a comma and the word "period" every time I want to end a sentence. I say "new paragraph" when I wish to start a new thought. I happily adjust my speech to the constraints of the machine, which is now enmeshed with my heavy breathing and the system of traffic lights on Manhattan's grid. I pause self-consciously for a moment as I'm describing the way I'm again speaking and am embarrassed when I recall a voice message that I left for a friend recently, where I said the words "comma" and "period" just as if I were speaking to Siri.

As I'm running, I'm also throwing off data to the cloud even though I don't wear a smartwatch or a fitness band. Instead, my phone is tracking every move my body makes and where I am. My Health app shows that I ran 4.49 miles today. In fact, my phone shows me every move I make in five-minute intervals all day long, every day. Today, for instance, from 5:05 to 5:10 P.M., I ran 0.5687 miles, whereas in the next five minutes, I ran 0.4918 miles. The app also shows me that I've taken 8,306 steps so far today and that on a typical day in 2015, I took 10,129 steps. And all of this information is stored deep in my privacy settings in the form of maps, which shows me gorgeously rendered visual representations of every single place I've been around the world over the past few years, along with the date and time I was there. On top of that, my phone's GPS is tracking every move I've made on this run and how fast I've been going. Since I've been running mostly in the streets, my data will be fed into the traffic reports on Google Maps. Since Google Maps can't tell whether I am in a car or running on the streets—to them, I'm just another pulsing GPS—my pathetic running speed will probably skew the results toward gridlock. Of course I am free to turn off these features but they're so buried I haven't bothered. I can assume that most of this data, if not all of it, is being sold to marketers and scooped up by government agencies like the NSA.

So my run, which I took to clear my head, is much more

complicated than I thought. I'm not just running; I'm throwing off an enormous amount of data, navigating the physical urban landscape, while structuring and writing my book. If I thought I was only doing one thing—running—I would be naïve. Even in my leisure, when strapped to a web-enabled device, I'm furiously multitasking and, in a very positive way, highly distracted.

Could we say that the act of running or walking in the city is what the act of speech is to language? Could we think of our feet as our mouth, articulating stories as we journey through the urban jungle? And in what ways are these stories written and communicated? When we walk, we trod upon a dense palimpsest of those who have traveled these same sidewalks before us, each inscribing on those pavements their own narratives. In this way, when we walk in the city, we are at once telling our own stories and retelling tales of those who came before us.

Walking the city invokes a text, one that is instantaneously written and read at once. The urbanist philosopher Michel de Certeau says, "They walk—an elementary form of this experience of the city; they are walkers, *Wandersmänner*, whose bodies follow the thicks and thins of an urban 'text' they write without being able to read it." Walking, then, is an act of reading the city with our feet. The city itself is an epic novel: each building a word, each street a sentence, and each block a paragraph. De Certeau's claim for unreadability is hinged on three facts: the blur of motion, the speed at which the tale is unwinding, and the sheer immensity of the text. When we speak of hypertexts, we usually mean those that exist online, but we might think of the city as the ur-hypertext, a dynamic, analog, predigital model of complex intertextuality.

In the twenty-first century, the story has entered a fourth dimension of data. As we walk, we emit streams of data, tracking where we're walking and how we're walking: how far, how fast, how many calories burned, and so forth. The air above the streets is thick with our narrative transmissions uploading to far-flung server farms where, parsed and analyzed, they reappear on our devices. We walk and we think; we read and we write. The rhythm of our walking influences the pace of our thinking. In a rush, we run/walk/think/read/write frantically and obsessively; at our leisure, casting aside logic, we let our feet instinctually caress the sidewalk's urban braille. Inspired by the surrealists, the situationists had a technique for urban sleepwalking that they called *dérive*, which literally translates as "drifting." Their idea was for the *dériviste* to completely give themselves up to the tugs and flows of the urban street, letting the crowds take them where they will, revealing regions of the city that, in their more "conscious" or "waking" moments, they would most likely not have been exposed to. Similarly, when beset by his demons, the painter Willem de Kooning would wander the dark streets of New York for most of the night, walking as far south as Battery Park at the southern tip of the island and then back. Often he went on these prowls alone, but friends occasionally accompanied him. The critic Edwin Denby said, "I can hear his light, tense voice saying as we walked at night, 'I'm struggling with my picture, I'm beating my brains out, I'm stuck.'" Relieving ourselves of intention, we get unstuck; drifting through the streets with a purposeful aimlessness, we find ourselves reading the city for pleasure.

When we drift through the city device-bound, we are enveloped in our own data storm, similar to the *Peanuts* cartoon character Pig-Pen, an embodiment of cloud-based computing. As a completely quantified being, each motion he makes—every step and every shake of the head—generates more visible dust. He doesn't traffic in clods of turf or thick mud. Instead, his dust is atmospheric and crystalline, melding with the air. Like snow, it gently falls on whatever it touches, only to be whisked away just as quickly. He's a machine; his cloud functions 24/7, continuously spewing billows of dust. Regardless of the weather, his condition remains unaffected; even rainstorms can't rinse him clean. His is a networked cloud, affecting those who come into contact with him; he himself is a living social network, always eliciting a strong interactive response from those in close proximity to him. Like a Wi-Fi signal in search of a smartphone, dirt finds Pig-Pen. Stepping outside after a bath, in clean clothes, he is immediately coated in dirt, declaring to Charlie Brown: "You know what I am? I'm a dust magnet!"

Wherever Pig-Pen walks, he is met with repulsion. His

critics—the entire cast of *Peanuts*—often accuse him of wallowing in his dirt, of taking a hedonistic pleasure in his condition. They say he's as self-absorbed and insensitive to others as he is a bastion of filth. But he sees it differently, claiming that he has affixed to him the "dust of countless ages." Deftly assuaging his critics, he turns the tables on them, forcing them to see value where before they saw none: "Don't think of it as dust," he says. "Just think of it as the dirt and dust of far-off lands blowing over here and settling on Pig-Pen! It staggers the imagination! I may be carrying the soil that was trod upon by Solomon or Nebuchadnezzar or Genghis Khan!"

As he moves through the world, he inscribes the contemporary into his cloud, adding the dirt of the day to his already thickly layered historical record. In this, he at once performs the roles of geologist, archeologist, and archivist. Like Homer, who transmitted his sagas orally, Pig-Pen is the bearer of a certain historical record, told in his own specific tongue. As an outcast, he assumes the role of the trickster, a figure who, defying normative community-based behavioral standards, is the keeper of a database of deep and secret knowledge. He is at once physical and ephemeral, omnipresent and local, site specific and distributed, time based and atemporal. His cloud is a haze, an ambience, a network that can't be defined by specific boundaries. It is without beginning and without end: a pulse, a stasis, a skein, a caliphate.

Going against the grain, his self-image is strong. Violet shows him a mirror and tries to humiliate him by asking,

"Aren't you ashamed?" Pig-Pen replies, "On the contrary. I didn't think I looked this good."

A few months later, on a cool autumn evening after work, I'm sauntering down Madison Avenue. I walk lockstep a few paces behind a woman who is thumbing her Facebook page as she languidly ambles. She is oblivious to anything else going on around her, including my shadowing her and looking over her shoulder. Like many of us, she has honed and fine-tuned her peripheral vision to animal strength, stopping with the crowds at corners, waiting for red lights, never looking up. When the lights change, she crosses the street, neither crashing into anyone nor stumbling on a curb. We walk together for about five or six blocks, at which point my attention is drawn to a man stopped dead still in the middle of the sidewalk texting. As a sea of pedestrians flow around him, he doesn't budge. He just stands there still as a stone. He's a human piece of street furniture, a public impediment to others—many of whom are also glued to their devices.

Everyone is in their own world, but it would be unfair to say that just because they aren't interacting with people on the street they're antisocial. In fact, they're aggressively social, but their interrelations are geographically distributed. Like sleepwalkers, they're both present and absent. I'm reminded of how the surrealists' ideal state for making art was the twilight between wakefulness and sleep, when they would dredge up images from the murky subconscious and poetically juxtapose them on the page or canvas. A few days later, I'm walking up Sixth Avenue with a buddy who almost collides with a digital sleepwalker. "Fucking zombies," he says, something I often hear used to describe them. He's right: "zombie" is an accurate way to depict our digital somnambulists. Zombies seem self-motivated, even purposeful, but it's an illusion. Completely lacking in awareness, zombies don't make choices. They're preprogrammed by drive, similar to the way consumers are. In fact, by nature, zombies are insatiable consumers. As reactivated corpses, zombies are living bodies rendered soulless, lobotomized by sorcery (which is itself a kind of programming), automated to consume living flesh.

It's been said that social media has turned us into ravenous consumerist zombies. Nothing has voracious brand loyalty the way social media does, which keeps us refreshing our feeds the way zombies crave flesh. On August 27, 2015, Facebook reported for the first time that one billion users logged on in a single day—and many of us compulsively log on several times a day. Each time we click Like on a status update we add to an already shockingly accurate profile of our consumerist selves—highly valuable information that's eagerly harvested by the network. Edward Snowden said that if we want to protect ourselves against government agencies scraping our data, we should get off Dropbox, Facebook, and Google and that we should "search for encrypted communication services" because they "enforce your rights." Few have taken his advice. Zombies can't be deprogrammed. The social media apparatus beckons us and we become addicted, joining the billion-plus strong for whom a life without social media is an impossibility. Social contacts, dating prospects, job opportunities, communications with loved ones—just about every interaction we have—flows through social media. For most of us it isn't a choice; it's a necessity. Even Snowden couldn't resist: on October 6, 2015, he joined Twitter.

Much of the web itself has been colonized by zombies that automatically churn pages, entice us to click on them, sometimes phishing for passwords, other times accumulating page views to generate ad revenue. At the same time, spiders—another type of zombie—crawl the web and consume all they can, indiscriminately sucking up files. Casting the widest net possible, they trawl data, passwords, and media that are warehoused in distant servers with the hopes of salvaging something of value, ultimately to be resold by yet more zombies. Every move we make on the web is tracked, transforming our digital peregrinations into data sets. Truly, our online lives—intersections of flesh and machine—are daily feasts of extreme digital consumption.

The zombies in George Romero's 1978 film *Dawn of the Dead*, were also hyperconsumers. Descending on a suburban shopping mall, they're doing all the things shoppers normally do—wandering aimlessly through the aisles, pushing their brimming carts to the piped-in strains of Muzak. A swarm of individuals who are unaware of each other, they act entirely out of self-interest. They are driven by the fierce desire to consume, in this case, the flesh of the living humans who have barricaded themselves inside the mall and who have also fallen prey to the dazzling array of products in this depopulated mall, all free for the taking. As much as the zombies have no real use for the consumer goods overflowing their shopping carts, neither do the humans. Trapped indoors, they can't play golf with their new shiny clubs or go anywhere fabulous in their recently liberated couture. Yet both—the humans and the zombies—are consumed by the act of consumption. And the human consumers may themselves ultimately be consumed—literally eaten—by the hyperzombie consumers.

Zombies replicate virally. Similar to the metrics of our social media accounts—your number of Twitter followers moves strongly in one direction—their numbers are always gaining in strength. Their power is in numbers: the more of them there are, the more powerful they are. Our power is also in numbers: the more followers we have, the more powerful we are. When we gain a follower, we don't gain a person; we gain a metric. And yet, many of our followers might in fact truly be zombies or bots—programs on a network that often appear to act and interact like humans—who follow us so we'll follow them back. A trick to swell our ranks is to buy followers, acquiring legions of zombies who will do our consuming on our behalf. Romero's zombie shoppers may have filled their shopping carts with stuff but they can't use it the same way you can't use all the data you download. However, someone else can: our computers are invaded by agents that turn them into zombies as part of a botnet—a swarm of bots—performing nefarious deeds without us even knowing it.

We are the walking dead, passive-aggressive, human-machine hybrids who are under the illusion that we're in control. But it's not that simple. We are collaborators with the zombies: sometimes wittingly, other times coercively, but always codependently. We are at once identified and self-identified with them, which might not be such a bad thing because the apparatus through which all of this flows—the network—is the ultimate zombie. The network appears to be more resilient than the waves of global epidemics and terrorism that continually engulf us. In spite of extremism, wars, mass migration, climate change, and market meltdowns in which fragile human bodies are decimated, our robust networks remain unbreakable in ways that bodies aren't.

A great inspiration for the dreamy surrealists was the nineteenth-century flaneur, an idle man-about-town who was the opposite of the zombie. Like a *dériviste* (the situationists also claimed the flaneur as a predecessor), he roamed the city alone, allowing himself to be pulled by the flows of the crowds on the grand boulevards. With no goal in mind, he was a spectator of the urban landscape, viewing the goings-on from the shadowy sidelines. Whereas the zombie was obsessed with consuming, the flaneur assiduously avoided it, feeling that to buy something would be too participatory. Instead, he was a world-class window-shopper, haunting enclosed arcades and narrow winding streets, browsing the displays. His was a stance of studied ambivalence. When asked about a certain topic of the day, he would feign indifference and recuse himself by simply saying, "I don't know" or "I don't care." The flaneur exemplified a position that Roland Barthes called "the neutral," wherein one intentionally places oneself in a state of uncertainty or indecision—living in a state between states—like sleepwalkers, ghosts, vampires, androids, and androgynous persons.* Neutrality was at the heart of the flaneur's resistance; fiercely individualistic, he resisted any attempts to be programmed or enlisted to join movements or groups. Uninterested in power, he was bereft of the kind of hungry desire that drives consumers and zombies.

The flaneur is hardwired into the ethos of the Internet: we "browse" the web with our "browsers," "surfing" from site to site, voyeuristically "lurking" from the sidelines. The digital flaneur obsessively frequents comment streams but doesn't dare leave a comment; he browses the great online shops and bazaars but doesn't buy anything; he googles

---

* The flaneur was always conceptualized as a "he," since during the nineteenth century, women were not able to walk around the city with the same freedom as men.

strangers but his online profile is studiously all but invisible. He is a peripatetic digital wanderer, pulled by the tugs and flows of his feeds, carelessly clicking from one spectacle to the next. Instagram is his Louvre, YouTube his Ziegfeld.

The flaneur has a buzzing, hovering presence, at once visible and unnoticed, not unlike the dozens of Wi-Fi networks crowded into the air we breathe. He is an embodiment of Marcel Duchamp's concept of the *infrathin*—a state between states. When asked to define the *infrathin*, Duchamp claimed it couldn't be defined, only described: "the warmth of a seat (which has just been left)" or "Velvet trousers / their whistling sound (in walking) by / brushing of the 2 legs is an / infrathin separation signaled / by sound." The *infrathin* is the lingering warmth of a piece of paper just after it emerges from the laser printer or the chiming start-up sound the computer makes, signifying its transition from death to life. When composer Brian Eno was commissioned to compose the Windows 95 start-up sound, he had to fulfill the requirements that it be "optimistic, futuristic, sentimental, emotional." He did that and more, coming up with a three-and-a-quarter-second pocket symphony. Eno, an artist familiar with Duchamp, invented an *infrathin* genre, "ambient music"—a hovering static music that is barely noticeable—which he intended to act as little more than an atmospheric perfume or tint to a room. The whooshing sound my e-mail program makes when I hit Send or the click of the shutter my smartphone makes when I take a picture are similarly displaced *infrathin* moments. These noises are signifiers of an event that in some ways happened and in other ways didn't happen. My mail was sent, silently and invisibly, and my photo was taken, but not in the way that I heard it. These series of contradictory events happening simultaneously—compatible and disjunctive, logical and absurd, present and absent, real and artificial—are evidence of ways in which the *infrathin* permeates our online lives.

The flaneur died with the birth of the department store. A creature of the boutiques, arcades, and streets, he felt unwelcome in the controlled confines of the big-box shops. His stage taken from him, the flaneur ceased to be. As the web becomes more commercial, I find I do less wandering than I used to. The web is now so riddled with zombies and their foul culture—clickbait, spam, ads—that I tend to return again and again to the few sites I know and trust. And even when I do, say, click to a site from a Facebook link, I find myself closing that window and returning to Facebook to seek another for fear that I, too, might become contaminated. Years ago, I might've hung around, exploring that site, drilling down to see what else was there, but today, the lure of social media draws me in over and over again, filling me with nostalgic sadness to witness my digital flaneur hovering on the verge of extinction.

Many lament the passing of the book's physicality. They are nostalgic for its smell, the sound of flipping pages, or the habit of dog-earing a page. But reading the web has a different type of physicality than reading on the printed page. When I click on a link, I literally press down on language, something that never happens when I'm reading a book. I find that when I read a web page, I tend to nervously mouse over the words I'm reading, highlighting them, pawing and dragging them around as I read. Sometimes when I read a book, if I'm reading really carefully, I'll run a finger over the words I'm reading; it's a surface engagement, which never actually transforms the words I'm reading, unlike when I highlight those same words with a yellow highlighter pen, physically altering them. Yet now when I highlight words on my iPad, I do so with the tip of my index finger. Same when I sign a tablet for a credit card charge with my finger. Relieving the need for an intermediary utensil, my flesh directly creates or alters words. In what way is this not physical? Even the resizing of images, which I do with my forefinger and thumb, physicalizes the way I interact with visual media, bringing to mind a popular YouTube video of a young child crying with frustration as she tries to enlarge a photograph in a print magazine by frantically moving her fingers back and forth.

We create the digital world in our own image. In this way, we can think of the web as a body double. With every click, we penetrate its flesh; with every bit of text we "cut," we incise its corpus. Page views are, after all, sometimes referred to as "impressions" or "hits" marking this body. The data trails we leave on it are inscribed, marked, and tracked, engraved in browser histories, clouds, and databases, like tattoos on that body. Attempts to cleanse that body range from plastic surgery for surface blemishes to invasive surgery to root out virally spreading cancers by companies such as reputation.com, whose slogan is: "We believe individuals and businesses have the right to control how they look online." In the European Union, one may exercise one's right to be forgotten, which allows you to have documents, recordings, or images of yourself scrubbed from the web so search engines don't index you, making you physically present and virtually absent, in essence, rendering you *infrathin*.

This sense of being in-between—being at once digital and physical—has spawned a reassessment of the relationship of our bodies to meatspace, the earthbound equivalent of cyberspace. There was a time when the divide between being online and off was clear. It used to be that when I was online, I was sitting at my desk, tied to a computer. During that time, I was clearly online. When I was done, I'd shut down my computer and take a walk around the block, being clearly offline. Today, I don't leave my house without a device; I'm still online when I take my walk around the block, smartphone in hand, at once straddling the physical and the virtual. In those days, the future appeared to be either/or. Either you were going to be spending time in sealed-off worlds like Second Life or Virtual Reality* or you'd be offline. Now

---

* While Facebook has invested heavily in the VR company Oculus, it's far from ready for prime time. *New York Times* reported during the 2016 CES show, "A decade from now, we may well look back on 2016 as the year virtual reality turned the corner from a futuristic novelty into a mainstream possibility." Farhad Manjoo. "On Display at CES, Tech Ideas in Their Awkward Adolescence." *New York Times*, January 6, 2016, p. B1.

wearable computing, mobile media, and augmented reality have reinscribed our bodies back into our physical settings, while we remain, at the same time, online. This intersection of the digital world and the physical has been driving the new aesthetic, a catchphrase cum art movement that was coined by the British designer James Bridle in 2011. No longer content to live exclusively on the screen, memes, images, and ideas born of digital culture are infiltrating and expressing themselves in meatspace. Think of digital pixelated camouflage as an example or a T-shirt with the dancing baby meme printed on it. This slight warping of reality, at once familiar and disconcerting, represents a shift in the ways we might process aesthetics much the same way Warhol's soup cans did, prompting author Bruce Sterling to comment: "Look at those images objectively. Scarcely one of the real things in there would have made any sense to anyone in 1982, or even in 1992. People of those times would not have known what they were seeing with those New Aesthetic images."

With technologies like augmented reality, geography itself has become unhinged from any singular verifiable, stable state, instead subjected to remixes and whimsical interpretations, overwashed with data-hazed layers of subjectivity, proposing the landscape itself as a series of collage elements to be repurposed and reconfigured. Standing in front of my apartment building on West Twenty-Sixth Street in New York City and looking at it through an AR app, I view not only the history of the building, a biography of the architect who built it, and the city records attached to it, but also a wealth of unofficial crowdsourced data lobbed on top of it: personal stories of births, deaths, breakups, love affairs, and memories. I can view photographs of these ghostly protagonists as readily as I can call up old pictures of the building. On top of this—if I'm using the unpaid version of the app— I'm seeing a stream of geogenerated advertising associated with my neighborhood: "Hill Country at 30 West Twenty-Sixth Street serves the best Texas-style ribs in the city" and "Duane Reade at Sixth Avenue and Twenty-Seventh Street is having a sale on shaving supplies today."

In this way, the twenty-first century itself feels both visible and invisible; the surface of things alone might be the wrong place to look. Instead, the physical mixed with the unseen—the *infrathin*—as expressed by those tiny devices in our hands or the thick data haze that permeates the air we breathe, is what locates us in the present. And in this way, the collapse of online and physical space functions as a marker, a moment that informs us that culture—along with its means of production and reception—has radically shifted beneath our feet while we were looking elsewhere.

The city streets, with their complex interplay of wakefulness and sleep, are rife with surrealism. Sometimes we barrel down the sidewalks apace, clinging to our devices; other times we meander slowly weaving in and out of the traffic flow as we stare down at our screens in a waking dream state. And yet, in the midst of the hustle and bustle, there are people actually sleeping in the teeming urban landscape around us. It's late at night, I'm walking down Broadway, and there, in a huge plateglass window facing the street, is a night watchman sound asleep. I stand directly in front of him—there's literally only a few millimeters of glass separating us—which is making my wife very uncomfortable. I ask her why and she responds, "You might wake him." I reply, "But he's sleeping, on display in public." Encased in glass, and looking very peaceful, he feels unwakable. It strikes me that the proportions of the glass, similar to a computer screen, have rendered him two-dimensional. Backlit, he looks like he's been flattened into a JPEG. The reflective surface of the glass and the flatness of the guard is creating a buzzy cognitive dissonance, making me feel as if I'm in the stylized world of *Grand Theft Auto* rather than on the gritty streets of New York. I snap a photo of him on my device. Gazing at the JPEG I just took, I see that he is now literally flattened into an image. I walk away from the scene with him in my pocket.

My wife's anxiety arises from the delicate play of public and private that happens on the streets of a crowded city. Walking down Fifth Avenue with a friend, we speak openly and loudly as if we were ambling down an isolated country lane. Yet many of us love to eavesdrop on these conversations, walking two steps in front or behind listening to these strangers' narratives unwind block after block. We do the same with people shouting into hands-free headsets. Once, the only people who spoke to themselves were drunks; today, armies of people spout great soliloquies whilst traversing the sidewalks.

Sleeping in public is an odd gesture. "Odd gestures of any kind are automatically taken as a threat," writes Paul Auster of urban life. "Talking out loud to yourself, scratching your body, looking someone directly in the eye: these deviations can trigger off hostile and sometimes violent reactions from those around you. You must not swagger or swoon, you must not clutch the walls, you must not sing, for all forms of spontaneous or involuntary behavior are sure to elicit stares, caustic remarks, and even an occasional shove or kick in the shins." Or else they're met with indifference, marking a person as crazy and dangerous; any interaction with them is potentially unpredictable. Our sprawling homeless population exudes a mixture of passivity and aggression: they sleep, sprawled out on curbs, in our midst; yet they panhandle those same corners. With the combination of these gestures, they pose a double threat, causing us to walk by them as if they're invisible. Addressing a packed house at Madison Square Garden, Pope Francis said, "In big cities, beneath the roar of traffic, beneath the rapid pace of change, so many faces pass by unnoticed because they have no 'right' to be there, no right to be part of the city . . . These people stand at the edges of our great avenues, in our streets in deafening anonymity." The oxymoronic term "deafening anonymity" has echoes of Eno's ambient music (unheard music) and Duchamp's *infrathin* (unnoticed phenomena), which accurately describes the homeless as flickering between two states, at once painfully visible and conveniently invisible.

I enter a subway car and see a man who is sound asleep. He's not laying down, but is sprawled across a few seats. He is emitting no odor and is dressed in reasonably clean clothes. He's neither sleep talking nor mumbling; he's just laying perfectly still, with the exception of his head, which sways in tandem with the jerks of the subway car. This is not a dangerous man; it is a sleeping man. Although the car is crowded, nobody will get near him. Oddly enough, almost everyone is huddled in the opposite end of the car, glued to their devices, replete with earbuds, in a state Breton would certify as being properly asleep (surrealistically speaking). While there are many seats available next to where the guy who is actually sleeping, the walking dead appear to have no desire to be anywhere near the authentic sleeper. I look at both parties and feel that in their own ways they each dreamily navigate the city in "deafening anonymity."

Sometimes I go to a big Korean spa in Queens. It's a wonderful lively place, filled with various pools and saunas. On weekends, it's particularly crowded, packed with families: noisy children shriek with joy as they run from one water feature to another. Amid the noise and chaos is a public sleeping area that is separated from the cafeteria only by a low sheetrock barrier. It's a large area, strewn with dozens of bodies of all sexes and ages, mostly clad in shorts, T-shirts, and bathing suits, all sound asleep. It's always very crowded, with sleepers cheek to jowl, lying perfectly still. In the midst of life, it's always surreal and lovely to see those lost in dream space among the waking.

It's past midnight, on our way home after seeing the sleeping guard in the window display, when I decide to invade someone's personal space. A woman is standing outside a bar texting. The street is empty and I slowly approach, staring down at my phone. I zombie walk lethargically toward her. I can feel her spying me out of her peripheral vision but she doesn't budge. I move closer. She stays where she is until I'm almost literally shoulder to shoulder with this total stranger. In times past, she might've been scared, or moved away, or called the cops. But now, with our devices in hand, she senses that I am no threat; zombies don't fear other zombies. She knows I am one of her own, much more interested in consuming my device than I am in consuming her.

CHAPTER 3

Our Browser History Is the New Memoir

The surrealists had a technique of constructing literature that they called "automatic writing," in which the poet or novelist sat down and, without conscious thought, put pen to paper and just started writing. The hand wrote, with the writer unaware of the meaning of what was being written. The hand continued to write on its own. Soon enough, if the writer were truly able to let go, the words would flow from deep within the subconscious to the page. Words always have meaning, the surrealists reasoned, so if you could give up intention, meaning would remain, but perhaps differently than you intended.

Could we think of our web browsing as another type of automatic writing? As we drift from site to site, our peregrinations are literally inscribed in our browser history. This is purely automatic writing, writing that writes itself. Let's say, I'm doing research for an article I've been writing for the past week or so. It's been a struggle to find just the right bits and pieces that will make the article really fly. Suddenly, I remember a line from something I read on the web a few days ago that just might be the thing I'm looking for. I try to google it, but the idea is rather germane and the words used to describe it are ordinary. The search gives me pages of results that aren't getting me anywhere. Suddenly, I have an idea: check my browser history. I crack it open, and after much scrolling, I locate exactly the page I was looking for. But as I'm scrolling through my history, I'm seeing my entire week flash before my eyes. It's a little bit embarrassing but there's my entire life—everything I was thinking about, curious about, angry about, desiring of—laid out before me. I had forgotten about most of this stuff—recipes for dinners that were never made, a pair of shoes that turned out to be too expensive, and a subsequent search to try to find them cheaper. I see the people who I stalked on Facebook, the videos I watched on Vimeo, and was embarrassed by how many times over the course of a week I self-googled. Since I spend so much of my time online, I was able to reconstruct pretty much my entire week in the most granular way. Can we think of our browser history as the new memoir, one that is being written automatically, effortlessly, unconsciously? If you want to know anything about me, what I was thinking, what I was interested in, exactly what I did or was going to do, check out my browser history: my passions, my hatreds, my crushes, my hopes—my intellectual and emotional life— all there before me, going back years and years, in all its embarrassment and all its riches.

My search history is astonishingly detailed: last Friday, between 11:00 A.M. and noon, for instance, it shows that I looked at forty-two different pages. And if I strung them together, I could literally reconstruct exactly what I was doing, what I was thinking about, and the associative patterns that my thoughts took during that hour. And that's just the time I was at my laptop. Chrome shows me my mobile browsing history from my phone and iPad as well, so not a click is missing. Gmail keeps an exact record of every correspondence I've had and social media tracks everything I've said, liked, or commented on. If I add the dozens of SMS messages I sent during that hour, then taken as a whole, I could reconstruct a fairly accurate self-portrait. And even if there were gaps, just glancing at a web page inscribed in my history can spark a chain of memories, enabling me to recollect thought patterns and reconstruct memories.

Buddhist meditators use a technique that they call mental noting. As each emotion arises, they give it a name: fear, excitement, sadness. They also assign names to sensations: coolness, warmth, pressure. They feel that naming things anchors the emotions, keeping the meditator in the present. It also helps distance themselves from the pull of those emotions so that they don't take on too much power, overwhelming the placidness of meditation. Noting is a way of making visible what is normally invisible, making something ephemeral concrete. Our browser history is doing exactly that and going further by not only naming, but also time-stamping and archiving these fleeting traces of data.

Our browser history could also be seen as a scrapbook,

a textual and visual travelogue. Fifty years ago, William S. Burroughs began using scrapbooks as mnemonic devices for his writing. When he read something in the newspaper that reminded him of something he'd written, he'd clip it and paste it into a scrapbook alongside the words from his book. Sometimes, when he'd be walking down the street and see a scene that reminded him of something he wrote, he'd take a picture of it, scrapbooking the photo alongside his text. He said, "I do a lot of exercises in what I call time travel, in taking coordinates, such as what I photographed on the train, what I was thinking about at the time, what I was reading and what I wrote; all of this to see how completely I can project myself back to that one point in time." Like surrealist techniques, the juxtaposition of related but disparate items were enough to kick off chains of richly associative thoughts and memories in Burroughs's mind.

Echoes of these ideas—digital and analog—can be found in two famous books written between the seventeenth and eighteenth centuries that are, in form and content, uncannily reminiscent of obsessive blogs or on active social media streams. One is the *Diary of Samuel Pepys* which was composed while Pepys was living in London, where he spent nine years—from 1660 to 1669—writing down every detail of his life and times. The diary totaled more than a million words and it's the best account of what it was like to live day to day in the seventeenth century; reading it can transport you back three centuries. While it gives firsthand accounts of historical events such as the Great Plague and the

Great Fire of London, it's also rife with juicy illicit personal details—many of which were enciphered using a shorthand mashup of several foreign languages—such as gossiping about friends and chasing women. The other book that gives us similarly granular details of the life and times in which he lived is James Boswell's biography, *The Life of Samuel Johnson, LL.D.*, a massive tome that is an accumulation of bits and pieces of the quotidian ephemera: letters, observations, patches of dialogue, and descriptions of daily life. Begun in 1763, when Johnson was fifty-four years old, it's not really a complete life of Johnson, but rather an intimate portrait of him over his final twenty-one years.

During that period, Johnson became great friends with a woman named Hester Thrale, who was half his age and had an intelligence to match his own. Though their relationship stayed platonic, Boswell became jealous of their friendship. Seven years after Johnson died, Boswell published his massive biography—my edition is more than 1,500 pages long—and when Thrale got her hands on the book, she was shocked by just how wrong Boswell got it. In her copy of the book, she started scribbling corrections and comments in the margins, such as [*absurd!*] or [*I don't recollect that*] and [*Johnson would not have liked to hear this of himself*]. By the time it was over, there were thousands of comments and annotations by Thrale in her copies of the book, which she turned into a small handmade edition, by obsessively scribbling marginal notes in one copy of the book after another, never changing her annotations from one copy to the next. Upon her death, her many copies were disbursed. One of them made its way to Boston and into the hands of poet Amy Lowell who, along with her pals, would spend nights howling with laughter at Thrale's bitchy comments. Thrale's trolling of Boswell is reminiscent, both in tone and combativeness, of the flame wars that erupt in web comment streams, and her self-publishing of her annotated editions was analog print on demand.

Can you imagine, were it possible, seeing Johnson's or Pepys's browser history? The weaving of small details into an account of a life was based on selective memory and subjective bias—as was pointed out by Mrs. Thrale—yet it's these exact qualities that give these works their eccentric literary charm. I excitedly think of the potential of a modern-day Boswell or Pepys scraping browser histories into a literary biography or memoir. Similarly, might we imagine Facebook as a grand experiment in collective cultural autobiography? For future sociologists, historians, and artists, social networking provides in detail a portrait of a civilization at a moment in time on a scale previously unimaginable in all its glory, and, truth be told, in all its ugliness.

In the early days of the Internet before social media, one of my students e-mailed himself things he wanted to remember. It could've been anything as mundane as a pair of sneakers he liked to a profound philosophical insight. Over the years, he never looked at these e-mails but he kept sending them to himself nonetheless. For his final project in my class, he went back to the first year he had done this and scraped all those e-mails, laid them out in a page-design program, and had a print-on-demand book made of them. He called it *Notes to Myself* after the best-selling self-help book from the 1970s by Hugh Prather. While the book wasn't interesting to anyone but himself, he cherished it as a diary, a physical embodiment of a time gone by, created with little effort or intention. His plan is to print out every year of those e-mails and collect them into a master set, one volume per year, a massive work of automatic autobiography. This furious accumulation of detail and data, from a creative point of view, is reason to celebrate. The vast amount of the web's language is perfect raw material for literature. Disjunctive, compressed, decontextualized, cut and pastable, and, most important, archivable, it's easily reassembled into works of art.

It's a beautiful early summer evening and a group of us are sipping wine on a terrace with a dramatic view overlooking the Adriatic Sea on the Dalmatian coast. It's dark and I can see the outline of the town below us hugging the rocky coastline, articulated by strings of streetlights. In the distance I can make out the dark shapes of mountains that melt into the sea as thousands of stars dot the ink-black sky. The various members of our group are chatting, drinking, and texting when suddenly, a giant peachy-yellow moon crests over the mountains in the distance. It's stunning and the

group goes silent as the moon quickly starts to rise—except
for one guy, who is glued to his phone, deep in a text conversation with his girlfriend. Our eyes keep moving from
the moon and then back to this guy. We can't believe he's
absorbed in his phone instead of being absorbed in the spectacular scene unfolding before our eyes. We're taking the ancient poet Basho's stance: "A haiku is like a finger pointing
to the moon / If the finger is bejeweled, we no longer see
the moon." And he's taking Marinetti's stance: "Let's mur-
der the moonshine." Finally, someone calls him out on it, to
which he responds, "I can see the moon anytime, but this is
the only time I can be having this conversation."

His remark gives me pause. He's right. Why is looking
at the moon somehow perceived to be more "present" than
looking at your phone? A specific text conversation happens
only once, whereas natural phenomena, while they don't always happen in such an extraordinary way as that moon, are
recurrent; wait around long enough and you'll see another
spectacular moonrise. It struck me that as much as we were in
the moment, so was he. Our moment wasn't better because it
was natural; it was simply different. It brings to mind an article I read about the practice of mindfulness, which stated,
"Mindfulness in its original Buddhist tradition is not about
being able to stare comfortably at your computer for hours on
end, or get 'in the zone' . . . it's about gaining insight into the
human condition." But don't programmers get in the "flow
state" all the time, spending hours in the hyperpresent? One
stray thought can lead to a wrong keystroke, botching a pro-

gram. I know typesetters, graphic designers, painters, musicians, and illustrators who are similarly mindful. In fact, it's hard to think of anyone deeply involved in work in front of a computer who isn't staring at a screen and completely in the moment. In regard to our texting friend, how is using a piece of technology to have a deep conversation with someone you love not insightful to the human condition?

Being fully present in the moment is what happens every time you load a web page. Web pages don't exist: they are spontaneously assembled at a split second's notice upon a click. They appear for a moment, then dissipate once that window is closed until called on again. A web page is comprised of a series of disparate codes from various places—sometimes on the same server, other times pulled from distant geographic locations—which pull images, RSS feeds, CSS, style sheets, and other bits of code to form a temporary constellation, which appears in your browser as a unified page. On dynamic sites—such as social media or news sites—those constellations are refreshed often, becoming fully new sometimes within seconds. The idea of a "dialectical constellation" comes from Walter Benjamin, who theorized that in order to study history we've got to be able to freeze a complex and dynamic stream of systems into a still moment. When this happens, he calls it a *"constellation"*: "It's not that what is past casts its light on what is present, or what is present its light on what is past; rather what has been comes together in a flash with the now to form a constellation"—which is a pretty good description of what happens when you click on a link, causing a web page to be spontaneously assembled. Similarly the Dada poet Raoul Hausmann wrote in his 1920 "Manifesto of PREsentism": "To compress all the possibilities, all the givens of every second into a tangible energy. Wisdom. Eternity is nothing. Let's seize each second today!"

Benjamin also wrote that "memory is not an instrument for exploring the past but its theater." If memory is but a stage set for events that once happened but can never be accurately and realistically recalled, then those props populating the stage must be stored somewhere after the play has ended. That space, in the twenty-first century, is the web. Ceding vast tracts of our memory to the web in the form of photographs, videos, and status updates that never vanish, we've created memory banks in finer detail than our brains are capable of conjuring. With the birth of hyperrealistic memory (a version of total recall through documentation) comes the death of poetic license and selective memory, upon which some of the greatest works of Western civilization—Proust and Nabokov come to mind—are built. Instead, in a time of information surplus, we find ourselves in a condition of "directed forgetting," the selective forgetting of outdated or irrelevant information in order to clear space for encoding new information on our brain's hard drive. Like a surveillance cam, information is being scrubbed as quickly as it is being written, keeping us in an eternal state of Hausmannian presentism.

Many decry the loss of "real time" to capturing moments on-screen, claiming that the recording of memories as they happen threatens to replace the actual memories you have of that moment. I've read many articles in which parents bemoan the fact their kids were seeing family vacations through GoPro cameras, rather than actually living them. After a day on the ski slopes, they edit their raw footage into action-packed greatest moments and post it to social media, where it's shared and commented on by their friends, hyperextending their time on the mountain. For a generation raised on reality TV to be able to replay those moments over and over through a mediated interface is a way of reliving an eternal present, loved for a moment then replaced by the next day's upload. In this way, we're simultaneously archiving and forgetting: archiving because we continuously upload media, and forgetting because we rarely go back to visit what we have uploaded. Today's upload is the best upload and keeps us very much present and mindful in the here and now.

The fear of outsourcing our memory to the web—known as "digital amnesia"—has ancient echoes. Plato was apprehensive about the transition from spoken language to the written word. He was fearful that those who wrote would stop exercising their memory and become forgetful; they'd rely on externalized graphical notation instead of their innate capacity to remember things. He derided writing as a *pharmakon* or substitute, a cheap imitation of speaking. As a result of writing, he feared knowledge would become information. Since there was no individual there to speak it—and speak for it—writing would literally dehumanize wisdom.

Speech, Plato felt, was high resolution and required full presence, whereas writing was low resolution and depended on absence. Memory was internal, writing external; speech carried the essence of knowledge, writing its appearance; spoken words were living, written marks were lifeless. We see similar fears in the digital age. Studies show that most people happily use the web as an online extension of their brains, and of those surveyed, half admit their smartphones are stand-ins for their memory.

Freud theorized rewritable memory when in 1925 he used a child's toy he called the "mystic writing pad" as a metaphor for the way human consciousness is structured. The pad consists of three layers: on the top there is a sheet of plastic, beneath there is a sheet of paper, and finally at the bottom there is a layer of wax. When you write on the plastic with a stylus, an impression is made both on the paper and on the waxy tablet. When you lift the paper up, the writing vanishes from it, but an impression is permanently embedded in the wax. Freud used this schema as a metaphor for how memory works: the stylus is the stimuli from the outside world, the two layers of plastic and paper are layers of consciousness, and the waxy bottom is the unconscious, where impressions are stored. Taken as an allegory for the digital age, the stylus is a metaphor for the material we're downloading (data), the paper and plastic are our data being currently used (random access memory or RAM), and the wax layer is the deep storage (read-only memory or ROM) of our hard drives or cloud computing, invisible but able to be recalled on command. The paper and plastic memories are dynamic and rewritable, while the wax is accumulative.

There are two seemingly contradictory temporal metrics happening on the web: the archival and the hyperpresent. How many times have we cynically noted that someone has shared something we'd already seen posted a month, a week, a day, or even an hour ago? Social media's architecture insists that everything always stays new. Facebook's web interface turns every link, literally, into a newspaper headline. A feature photograph is captioned by a headline in large serif type, reminiscent of Times Roman, underneath which is a line of descriptive text in a smaller sans serif font. Below that, in all caps, but with a lighter font, is the name of the website. The entire link is bounded by a thin, one-pixel rule, making it feel just like an item in a newspaper. The result of this is that every link posted to Facebook, no matter how big or small, trivial or important, gives the sense that it's breaking news: Bored Panda has the identical visual weight and import as the *Washington Post* online. Social media's genius is its leveling quality: every voice has the same volume and every link is an urgent call to action. It keeps us glued: blink for a moment and you might miss something important.

The faster things get, the slower they become. In the midst of this dynamism, we are simultaneously archiving elements of each page in our browser's cache. Similarly, when I'm reading on a device, every move I make—from my "page turns" to the speed at which I'm reading—is tracked and sent to a database, converting the fleeting experience of reading into something quantified. Automated spiders are also reading the web, silently and continuously. For them—the most voracious readers in history—reading is literally archiving as they indiscriminately index every word without ever "reading" any of it. The ecology of the web teeters on the cusp of the hyperpresent and the eternal: Just think of the legions of sites built for now-expired academic conferences or weddings that long ago ended in divorce that eternally linger, visited only by the occasional spider, who, sucking the dead data from these corpses, imprisons it in distant digital ossuaries.

While we have the illusion that things are speeding up, they've actually reached a point of stasis, of stillness. The technology theorist Paul Virilio claims that "there is a definite relationship between inertia and absolute speed which is based on the stasis which results from absolute speed. Absolute stasis leads—potentially—to absolute stasis." When the speed of information moves at the speed of light, as it has with our fiber optic networks, accelerationism has bumped up against its speed limit, thereby ceasing to be accelerationist. Instead, it is static, signifying the end of the technological narrative of speed and the inevitable beginning of another: entropy.

CHAPTER 4

Archiving Is the New Folk Art

Of all the things known about Andy Warhol, the fact that he curated a show called *Raid the Icebox 1* at the Rhode Island School of Design Museum in Providence in 1969 is one of the more obscure. In fact, combing my shelf of books by and about Warhol (twenty-eight in total), there's not a single mention of it. It's strange because, living his life as a celebrity under the glare of the media, not a moment was otherwise missed.

Back in the 1960s, Warhol traveled in wealthy circles and his great patrons John and Dominique de Menil had strong connections to the RISD Museum's young director, Daniel Robbins. While trying to raise some funds for the museum, Robbins gave the de Menils a tour of the museum's vast storage spaces, where they were wowed by the treasures that were languishing far from the public's view. Many of the objects were in poor condition and so they hatched a fundraising scheme, which involved inviting a hip artist into the storerooms to curate a show. The artist they chose was Andy

Warhol. They had no idea what they were getting into. In short, it was a total disaster.

Warhol treated the museum as if he were on a shopping spree at a flea market, grabbing everything he could—shoes, umbrellas, blankets, baskets, chairs, paintings, pottery—and then casually displaying them in the museum. The paintings were stacked on top of each other the way they are in a thrift shop; the antique shoes were crammed into cabinets, vaguely resembling Imelda Marcos's closet; the nineteenth-century parasols were hung from the ceiling, looking like a cross between slumbering bats and a surrealist assemblage; gorgeous colonial chairs were piled atop each other like in a cafeteria about to be cleaned; colorful Navajo blankets were stacked on top of a cheap table as if they were in a department store, with the cardboard boxes they came in shoved beneath the table. And that's just the beginning.

The museum's curatorial staff was offended by what they perceived to be Warhol's irreverence in handling their treasures. They saw his choices as indiscriminately lazy and his presentation as preposterous. What's more, Warhol demanded that only fake paintings be shown. "If that's real," he said, pointing to a Cézanne still life, "we won't take it." They thought Warhol was truly the ignoramus his public persona pretended to be. Hindsight is twenty-twenty. Over the next forty-five years, the art world would mold itself to Warhol's vision, celebrating commodities, the market, and consumer excess. His own studio work also explored excess: Why make only one Brillo box when the supermarket has a stack? Why paint only one portrait of Ethel Scull when you can charge her for thirty-six? To a poor kid from the Pittsburgh slums, *more* was always better. And after Warhol's death, *more* was what they found in his Upper East Side townhouse, which was crammed to the gills with unopened boxes of coats, watches, diamonds, rugs—you name it— piled up in rooms so stuffed you could barely enter them. In 1988, a year after he died, all of Warhol's possessions were laid out for all to see on huge tables at Sotheby's in New York: the whole thing—ten thousand items, from cookie jars to precious gems—eerily resembled *Raid the Icebox 1*.

But why should we care now? There's something about Warhol's obsessive cataloging and collecting, his archiving and displaying, that resonates in the digital age. Many of us raid the digital icebox every day, downloading more cultural artifacts than we know what to do with. I think it's fair to say that most of us have more MP3s sitting on our hard drives than we'll ever be able to listen to, and yet we keep acquiring more, not so different from the way Warhol hoarded cookie jars or delighted in displaying the dozens of pairs of shoes he found at the RISD Museum. In some ways, Warhol seems to be saying that quantity is more important than quality; it doesn't matter what you have as long as you have a lot of it.

You could say that in the digital age, with its free flow and circulation of cultural artifacts, that the act of acquisition— raiding the digital icebox—has turned many of us into amateur curators and archivists. We dig into the deep reserves of the web and arrange them, sometimes for a public (file sharing, MP3 blogs) and sometimes for oneself (the joys of collecting), and like Warhol, often for the sake of gathering itself. In this way, older arts of compiling such as commonplace books and scrapbooking have reemerged, inverting the predominant form of top-down cultural consumption of the twentieth century, when collections would consist as often of things bought—an LP or book—as things found. On the web, circulation has surpassed ownership: someone owns a material artifact, but who owns a JPEG? Commonplace books and scrapbooks combined democratic-based practices such as crafts, folk arts, and hobbies with the avant-garde tradition of the *objet trouvé*—found objects admired for their aesthetic qualities—which resonates with our current obsessions of archiving, arranging, hoarding, and sorting of digital readymades.

When asked, "How do you choose a readymade?" Duchamp replied, "It chooses you, so to speak." One can imagine Duchamp drifting into the plumbing supply and letting the urinal choose him, one object among many lodged in a protosurrealist *wunderkammer*, unbelievably rich in its limited offerings. I think we can relate. How many times have we wandered into a record store, boutique, or bookstore and let objects choose us? In this way, Duchamp collapsed the distinction between artist and shopper and added a dash of surrealism. Yet if we really gave ourselves over to Duchamp's procedure and let objects choose us as we browsed the web, surely we'd be overwhelmed by the sheer number of artifacts. To manage the vastness, we employ guided chance via search engines. Let's say I'm looking for a specific image. To wait until it found me—in Duchampian terms—would be ludicrous. Instead, I plunk my term into Google Images search and *then* let one of them choose me. In this way, the web is a push and pull of opposites: intuition and intention, conscious and unconscious, drift and determination.

The play of conscious and unconscious is extended into the structure of the web itself. We could say that the mechanics that runs the web—from the code to the server farms—are the web's subconscious, while the software—the graphical user interface and all the activities that happen there, on the surface—is the web's consciousness. The unconscious, which is pure apparatus, is all hung on a grid, starting with binary code, moving to the pixel, and resulting in GUIs (graphical user interfaces). In this way, the web is an extension of modernism, reiterating a stasis that Rosalind Krauss claimed to be the hallmark of modernity: "The grid announces, among other things, modern art's will to silence, its hostility to literature, to narrative, to discourse." As an apparatus, the web is grid-like: static and even-keeled, a state more than a thing. On top lies a thin layer, the web's "content," which Krauss refers to as "literature, narrative, and discourse." All of the image archiving interfaces—Pinterest, Flickr, Instagram, Google Images—are gridded, from the rectangular format of the images to the lattices on which they are hung. While the images themselves may proffer organic subject matter, the interface and apparatus is entirely industrial. When we use an apparatus extensively, it becomes invisible, as we become completely subsumed by content. In 2000, the media theorist Matthew Fuller wrote an essay addressing the dangers of this exact blind spot; the title of his essay was "It Looks Like You're Writing a Letter: Microsoft Word." A decade and a half later, we still take apparatus for granted, the way we might take breathing or our body's circulatory system for granted; clearly, it's what makes everything function, but when I look in the mirror, all I can think about is how I need a haircut.

Pinterest is a human-driven image-harvesting engine, one that is fast becoming the largest single-source image repository on the web. When you pin an image from the web for one of your boards, Pinterest copies it to its own servers, providing you with a thumbnail and a link back to its original source. Therefore, should an image disappear from, say, a shuttered blog, it will remain on your Pinterest board. In this way, Pinterest is acting as an image redundancy and archive service, while at the same time building a vast proprietary image library. Because each image archived is pinned by human librarians, the signal-to-noise ratio is high as compared to Google Images, which are culled algorithmically. The darker side is that every user is ultimately working for Pinterest; with each pin, the company's image database grows richer—as does the corporation's bottom line.

Pinterest is Duchampian in that users don't generate any original content; instead, all images are drawn from elsewhere on the web. As opposed to Flickr or Instagram, every photo on Pinterest is a ready-made or a collage of preexisting images. To achieve this, the site uses a data compression algorithm called deduplication, which is a way of reducing the size of images by outsourcing redundant chunks of data to a single file that can be inserted into an image on demand. So, let's say that I've pinned an image of a dog with brown eyes. Housed in the Pinterest database is an untold number of photos of dogs with brown eyes. The algorithm scans all of those eyes and determines that in many cases portions of the pixel configurations are identical. So when I load my dog, the algorithm shoots a reference with that exact pixel set and inserts it where my dog's eye is. My dog, then, is not a photograph of a dog in the traditional sense but instead is patched together from a database of preexisting elements on the fly. Each image is at once both unique and cloned, reverberating with modernism's constructivist methods of collage and assemblage, as well as postmodernism's mimetic strategies of appropriation and sampling.

But Pinterest's emphasis on found and assembled materials also leads right back to the premodern notions of collecting and scrapbooking, which is no coincidence since the company claims that the platform is "built by hobbyists, for hobbyists" and that one of the partners' "boyhood bug collection is the touchstone inspiration and the company's founding myth." Walter Benjamin, an obsessive collector himself, wrote about the close connection between collecting and making when he said, "Among children, collecting is only one process of renewal; other processes are the painting of objects, the cutting out of figures, the application of decals—the whole range of childlike modes of acquisition, from touching things to giving them names." Pinterest's CEO has described the site as a "catalog of ideas," which echoes Benjamin's idea that "if there is a counterpart to the confusion of a library, it is the order of its catalog." Pinterest's apparatus converts the confusion of an image library into an order of a searchable catalog. While the users of Pinterest curate photo albums, the algorithms are the librarians, bots that sort the profusion of content.

The alt-librarian Rick Prelinger has proclaimed archiving as a new folk art, something that is widely practiced and has unconsciously become integrated into a great many people's lives, potentially transforming a necessity into a work of art. Now, at first thought it seems wrong: how can the storing and categorizing of data be folk art? Isn't folk art the opposite, something predicated on the subjective handcrafting of an object into a unique and personal statement, oftentimes one that expresses a larger community ethos? One need think of, say, the magnificent quilts of Gee's Bend produced over many generations by a group of African American women who live in an isolated Alabama town. Each quilt is unique, while bearing the mark of that specific community. Or the spectacular cosmic visions of someone like Rev. Howard Finster, whose obsessive, emotional, hand-rendered religious paintings and sculptures could only be sprung from the unique genius of Finster himself.

Like quilting, archiving employs the obsessive stitching together of many small pieces into a larger vision, a personal attempt at ordering a chaotic world. It's not such a far leap from the quilt maker to the stamp or book collector. In the digital age, our relentless "pinning" of images on Pinterest, curating of Instagram feeds, or compiling of Spotify playlists are contemporary expressions of folk archiving, ones that hearken back to predigital technologies. Pinterest's main metaphor is the cork-lined bulletin board, itself a site of folk archiving, which John Berger wrote about in his 1972 book *Ways of Seeing*:

> *Adults and children sometimes have boards in their bed-rooms or living-rooms on which they pin pieces of paper: letters, snapshots, reproductions of paintings, newspaper cuttings, original drawings, postcards. On each board all the images belong to the same language and are all more or less equal within it, because they have been chosen in a highly personal way to match and express the experience of the room's inhabitant. Logically, these boards should replace museums.*

In this passage, Berger positions the folk art of scrap-booking as high art, but the two have long been intertwined. Many artists in their studios have inspiration boards, not too different from what Berger is describing, pinned with postcards, inspirational notes, photographs, and so forth. And in the twentieth century, many libraries had "clipping libraries," where cabinets were bursting full of photographs clipped from magazines, glued to cardboard backings, and arranged by subject. Berger's deduction regarding the obsolescence of museums rings true for many; Pinterest's images are more integrated into their daily lives than the occasional visit to the museum is. For many, the postcard or JPEG, in essence, has become the painting.

The founder of *Whole Earth Catalog*, Stewart Brand, has stated that "like everything else, [curating] has been democratized by the Net, in one sense, everybody is curating: whether you are writing a blog, it is curating . . . So we are becoming editors, and curators, and those two are blending online." Even something as simple as bookmarking kicks off a chain of curation. When I instapaper a long-form article so I can read it later, it is added to my archive of articles. Oftentimes, due to the fact that things disappear from the web, if it's an article I think is particularly worthwhile, I'll convert it to a PDF and save a copy of it in my articles archive on my computer, creating my own personal library. As many users of MP3 blogs, file locker services, and streaming services know all too well, things vanish all the time. Sometimes users kill their blogs; other times, as in the case of Netflix, studio contracts expire, resulting in the disappearance of specific films, or regional geographical differences make their service unavailable in various countries. I went to a conference in China a few years ago where several of the conferees "brought" their papers on Google Docs, only to find out that once they arrived in mainland China, Google was blocked. Same with their Gmail, Twitter, Facebook, and YouTube. And as much as Wi-Fi is ballyhooed, it's still locked down in many places, making it less than reliable. Creating a robust local archive of digital artifacts is perhaps the most effective means by which to protect yourself against cloud-based instability.

Our archiving impulse arises as a way to ward off the chaos of overabundance. And yet even in the predigital age, the collector could never actually consume the sheer volume of cultural artifacts that could be collected. Anatole France (1844–1924), for instance, when asked of his vast library, "You have read all these books, Monsieur France?" answered, "Not one-tenth of them. I don't suppose you use your Sèvres china every day?" The condition of too much far precedes the nineteenth, twentieth, and twenty-first centuries. René Descartes (1596–1650) claimed that "even if all knowledge could be found in books, where it is mixed in with so many useless things and confusingly heaped in such large volumes, it would take longer to read those books than we have to live in this life." The Harvard historian Ann Blair relates how Kant (1724–1804) and Wordsworth (1770–1850) were among the earliest authors who described an experience of temporary mental blockage due to "sheer cognitive exhaustion . . . whether triggered by sensory or mental overload." Blair charts the rise of various indexing systems—as well as the invention of commonplace and reference books—as a way to order the impending chaos of overproduction and underconsumption. And like today, the ever-accumulating knowledge and the various attempts to manage it was felt globally across the centuries, from medieval/early modern Europe to the Islamic world and China.

The managing and sorting of information became an industry hinged on the illusion of control, which grew alongside increasingly codified systems of knowledge and rhetoric. Eventually, it evolved into a booming and lucrative industry, with the rise of everything from Johnson's *Dictionary*—for which he was paid roughly the equivalent of $350,000 in today's money—to the current crop of paywalled archives such as LexisNexis, ProQuest, and JSTOR, for which academic institutions spend between $10 billion and $20 billion annually. Information—who produces it, who consumes it, who distributes it, and, in short, who controls it—has been a contested space for centuries. While this is nothing new, when placed in the replicating digital ecosystem of the Internet—with its array of pirate and legitimate venues—these tendencies go into overdrive, creating new and unintended consequences in a variety of related areas such as copyright, intellectual property, historical contextualization, free culture, archiving, taxonomies, distribution, artistic practices, and curating, to name but a few.

Prior to the digital age, a common metric for expressing the infinite was the Argentinian writer Jorge Luis Borges's short story "The Library of Babel" (1941), which imagines a vast library that contains every book that could be written about every subject known to mankind. But one problem with Borges's library was information management—finding anything was nearly impossible. In his story, such drudgery was ceded to teams of weary human librarians who perished in their lifelong efforts to locate specific books in the labyrinthine library. And yet Borges was an optimist: with the right combination of fortitude and luck, there was a chance that a librarian could overcome the greatest odds; even though it's vast, his library is not infinite. And there are no duplicate copies of any books; every book is unique. But the problem is that many books are nearly identical, differing only in a single letter or a comma. Somewhere in that library, still yet to be found, would be one book that could contain all the world's knowledge between its covers printed in minuscule type and on an infinite number of infinitely thin leaves. That book of books—the Library of Babel—turned out to be the Internet.

A twenty-first-century version of Borges might resemble an author named Philip M. Parker, who, with the help of computers, has churned out more than a million books on a wide range of arcane subjects. When someone wants to buy a book of his, an army of spiders is sent out to crawl the web for content. Upon being hauled in, algorithms determine and sequence the most relevant information. They are then assembled into books (slightly shifting the semantic order to avoid direct plagiarism), chunked into predetermined print-on-demand formats, and automatically posted to Amazon, where titles are fabricated only if someone wants to buy the book. The process is so automated that titles are listed that haven't yet been written; if someone desires to have a book written on any subject, it is produced for them on demand. Parker's is but one of many such projects, where perfectly semantic accounts of sporting events and financial transactions are generated from generic data sets and published in newspapers all over the world; no one has any idea that there isn't a human writing these things. Both Parker and Borges play down content and quality, choosing instead to focus on quantity and the challenge of wrangling meaning—and in the case of Parker, money—out of such vastness.

Today we're confronted with the abstraction of big data—large data sets, expressed in equally large and equally abstract numbers—and it's assumed somehow that we can comprehend these. For instance, the WikiLeaks site contained 1.2 million documents a year after it was launched; and in 2010, it released almost 400,000 documents related to the Iraq War alone. The United States diplomatic cable leaks totaled 251,287 documents consisting of 261,276,536 words. A common complaint was that WikiLeaks released *too* damn much, prompting the journal *Foreign Policy* to call the release of such a vast amount of data "information vandalism":

> There's a principle that says it's OK to publish one-off scoops, but not 250,000—or for that matter 2.7 million—of them all at once? The former feels like journalism; the latter seems

grotesque and irresponsible, more like "information van-
dalism" . . . And even if responsible papers like the New
York Times *have a chance to review and contextualize*
them, there's no way they can dot every i *and cross every* t
in the time allotted. There's just too much.

And with every new leak, comes a new metric of immensity: it is said that Edward Snowden initially leaked between 1.5 and 1.7 million documents.

To give an idea of how much this is, in 1969, the conceptual artist On Kawara (1933–2014) embarked on a project
entitled *One Million Years*, which was a twenty-volume set
of books that printed the name of each year in closely type-
set columns (1856 AD 1857 AD 1858 AD, etc.). Each page
contains five hundred years, and each book contains 2,068
pages. As an absurdist gesture, live readings of the work are
occasionally given; the complete reading of the years could
never be finished in one's lifetime. If recorded, 2,700 CDs
would be needed to complete the readings; if read aloud, it
would take a hundred years to enumerate aloud the names of
one million years.

Too much was the same accusation that drove the young
hacktivist Aaron Swartz to take his life after being hound-
ed by the United States Department of Justice for attempting to liberate approximately 4.8 million articles (or seventy
gigabytes) from JSTOR, the paywalled academic database.
It's hard to imagine exactly what constitutes, say, 10,000
documents let alone 250,000 or 5 million. And yet it's this

metric that is propelling public discourse, not to mention legal policy. The immensity of the digital is hard to imagine. I shudder to think what my apartment would look like if every MP3 and PDF on my drives were to manifest itself as an album or a book, or if every video on my hard drive were somehow converted to film stock, wound on reels. I wouldn't be able to move. Each day, as we shuffle our data from one place to another, we have the illusion of mastery, when in fact we are drowning in our own riches. Our data— the management, storage, organizing, and moving of it— owns us. Ask anyone who's had to maintain a blog, Facebook page, or Twitter account: it's a second job. In effect, many of us have unwittingly become both the authors of Borges's "Library of Babel" and its lowly librarians.

I began to get curious about what *immensity* might look like and went in search of Swartz's cache, which—predictably locked down by the Department of Justice—was nowhere to be found. However, a tribute action dedicated to Swartz the day after his arrest in 2011 appeared on the Pirate Bay in the form of a thirty-three-gigabyte torrent that consisted of 18,592 PDFs from the *Philosophical Transactions of the Royal Society*, a prestigious scientific journal with a history extending back to the 1600s that was illegally downloaded from JSTOR and posted publicly by a user named Greg Maxwell. The torrent was accompanied by a free culture statement, which, in part, read: "This archive . . . should be available to everyone at no cost, but most have previously only been made available at high prices through paywall gatekeepers like JSTOR. Limited access to the documents here is typically sold for $19 USD per article, though some of the older ones are as low as $8. Purchasing access to this collection one article at a time would cost hundreds of thousands of dollars."*

A day later, upon unzipping one of the many files, I was faced with an overwhelming number of PDFs, ranging from 1 to 254 pages long. I couldn't absorb more than the smallest fraction of what I had just downloaded—and what I had just downloaded was but a fraction of the 4.8 million documents that Swartz had liberated. The sheer size of this smallest corner of the Internet verged on a cosmic scale. This scale itself is an abstraction: certainly we can't conceive of what Swartz's 4.8 million "articles" might look like, never mind what we would do with them were we to actually have them in our possession. It seems that all we know for sure is that Swartz downloaded *a lot*. Maxwell's gesture is at once a ghost of, and at the same time the only concrete realization of Swartz's vision, one that is both symbolic and instructive. No one will ever read Maxwell's trove (same with Swartz's), but the fact of this material—and, in Maxwell's case, its ever-present availability—competes with what practical applications we might render from it. The media critic Darren Werschler feels that content might be the wrong place to look for meaning:

---

* JSTOR eventually made these files free for public download.

It feels like the end of the modernist notion of "informa-
tion." Modernity brought with it the idea that there was
this thing that could be extracted that represented the most
valuable part of a text. Swartz's gesture suggests that there's
no "information" in places like JSTOR and Elsevier. Any
paper is as good as any other for a gesture like his, because
individually these papers literally have NO audience—an
average academic paper is read by maybe two or three peo-
ple. So the gesture only matters when it's done in bulk and
it doesn't matter of what the bulk consists. The offense is a
corporate one; it has relatively little to do with individual
authors because it assumes from the outset that the individ-
ual author isn't all that important.

Aaron Swartz's gesture was a conceptual one, focused
on the power of making available sealed-off information. He
wasn't concerned with what he was liberating; he was interested in using the model of moving masses of information
as a political tool, as if to say that the gesture of furiously
pushing, moving, gathering, sharing, parsing, storing, and
liberating information is as important as what's actually being moved.

In 2010, Pamela Echeverria, owner of the LABOR gallery
in Mexico City, held a conference called Who Owns the Im-

age? that focused on the way images and their reception have
been changed by digital culture. Echeverria, like so many of
us, was living a double life: on one hand, she dealt in unique
fine art objects at the gallery; on the other hand, she was
downloading scads of infinitely reproducible artifacts from
file sharing. The conference sparked numerous heated conversations, many of which Echeverria and I continued to discuss long after the conference ended.

In early 2013, shortly after Aaron Swartz passed away,
Pamela asked me to curate a show dedicated to his memory
at her gallery. When I began working on the show, I pon-
dered the sort of immensity that Swartz and Assange (and
later Snowden) were dealing in. What would it look like if
their leaks were somehow materialized? And how would it
make us think differently about them if we could physically
comprehend their magnitude? With a more conventional exhibition in mind, I began by seeking artworks that explicitly
sought to concretize digital data into physical objects. For
instance, I discovered a huge book that consisted of every
photograph of Natalie Portman on the Internet. I also found
a series of twelve books that recorded all changes made to
the Wikipedia article on the Iraq War; the volumes covered
a five-year period from December 2004 to November 2009,
with a total of twelve thousand changes. The set of books
was nearly seven-thousand-pages long. Along similar lines,
I came across a piece by an Iraqi American artist that was a
collection of every article published on the Internet about
the Iraq War, bound into a set of seventy-two books, each a

thousand pages long. Displayed on long tables, they made a stunning materialization of the quantity of digital culture.

But somehow these gestures, although big, were not big enough. They were too precious, too boutique, and too small to get at the magnitude of huge data sets that I was seeking to replicate. I wondered how I could up the ante. The Iraq War books showed that printing out even a small corner of the Internet was an insane proposition. My mind made a poetic leap: what if I were somehow able to crowdsource printing out the *entire* Internet?

I leapt on social media and put out a call:

LABOR, UbuWeb, and Kenneth Goldsmith invite you to participate in the first-ever attempt to print out the entire Internet.

The idea is simple: Print out as much of the web as you want—be it one sheet or a truckload—send it to Mexico City, and we'll display it in the gallery for the duration of the exhibition, which runs from July 26 to August 31, 2013.

The process is entirely open: If it exists online and is printed out, it will be accepted. Every contributor will be listed as a participating artist in the show.

What you decide to print out is up to you: As long as it exists somewhere online, it's in. We're not looking for creative interpretations of the project. We don't want objects. We just want shitloads of paper. We're literally looking for folks to print out the entire Internet. We have over 500 square meters of space to fill, with ceilings that are over six meters high.

There are many ways to go about this: You can act alone (print out your own blog, Gmail inbox, or spam folder) or you could organize a group of friends to print out a particular corner of the Internet, say, all of Wikipedia, the entire New York Times *archive, every dossier leaked by WikiLeaks for starters. The more the better.*

Print out the Internet. Post it to Mexico City.

At the conclusion of the show, the entire archive will be recycled.

The response was overwhelming. More than twenty thousand submissions poured in from every corner of the globe, manifesting themselves in a ten-ton heap of paper that was nearly five meters high. The pile looked a lot like the Internet itself, crammed with spam, credit card reports, memes, in-boxes, news sites, and porn—lots and lots of porn. Overnight, countless blogs and international media outlets ricocheted the idea across the globe, sparking intensely negative reactions, accusing me of everything from igniting an arboreal holocaust to cynical careerism. An online petition sprung up pleading: "Kenneth Goldsmith, please don't print the Internet," which petered out at less than five hundred signatures. The project grew so furiously that in July 2013, it was made an official meme on the website Know Your Meme. By the time it was over, more than a thousand pages of commentary had been generated—ironically, making a thousand more pages of the web that needed to be printed and thrown onto the pile. As most people never made it to Mexico City to see the actual show, the idea itself and the conversation it generated became a stand-in. Fueled by rumor and hearsay, the pile of papers grew to monumental proportions in the public's mind. It's fair to say that the conversation around the show was more real than the show itself.

As speculation about the project grew, I couldn't help but wonder what made people actually take something so ridiculously impossible so seriously? If you stopped even for a moment to think about it, printing the entire Internet is simply impossible. How can one even define the Internet, never mind freeze it for a moment to be able to print it? In the time it took me to write this sentence, an untold number of new web pages were generated, never mind the gajillions of photos, videos, and music that were just uploaded—each expandable to miles of source code, which in alphanumeric terms would mean oodles and oodles more pages. Trying to print out the entire Internet sounds like punishment meted out on a Promethean scale. The alarms tipped to near hysteria, resembling a twenty-first-century version of Dutch tulip mania more than the supposedly logical, levelheaded, contemporary world we imagine we live in.

Printing out the Internet was a physical manifestation of every skeleton in our digital closet, tumbled out, and splayed across the floor, pushing us out of house and home, forcing us to confront the fact that we are hoarders of the worst sort, even if that hoarding is now invisible. Printing the Internet was a grade-B zombie film, a cheap version of *War of the*

Worlds, the return of the repressed, a physical expression of the irrational fear that all this stuff will one day come back to haunt us. I'd like to believe that *Printing Out the Internet* was an unarticulated fear of abundance, of *too much*, of trying to comprehend a scale so large that no human brain could process it. Instead, we needed to invent, imagine, and enact the smallest slice of this problem in order to even contemplate purging ourselves of it.

The project was a slanted and swerved tribute to Aaron Swartz, filtered through the poetic lens of Jorge Luis Borges. It was a fleeting "dialectical constellation" of the Internet, materialized and frozen for a moment in a gallery in Mexico City, only to be blown apart, pulped, recycled, and reconstituted into some other form. The outcry from the public was misplaced, having demanded real solutions to what was an imaginary problem—imaginary because it never really happened. What happened instead was a global conversation about a proposition—a tear in the curtain—one of those strange moments when strands of magical realism, pataphysics (the science of imaginary solutions to imaginary problems), and meme culture collided, fleetingly materialized, and just as quickly vanished from the face of the earth.

In his introduction to his short story collection *Ficciones* (1941), Borges wrote: "The composition of vast books is a laborious and impoverishing extravagance. To go on for five hundred pages developing an idea whose perfect oral exposition is possible in a few minutes! A better course of procedure is to pretend that these books already exist, and then to offer a résumé, a commentary . . . I have preferred to write notes upon imaginary books." It's no surprise that both "The Library of Babel" and "Pierre Menard, Author of the *Quixote*"—in which an author spontaneously re-creates *Don Quixote* word for word, having had no prior knowledge of the book—appear in this collection. Textuality is objectified, not to be tampered with, frozen into baubles to be handled either by librarians or duplicate authors. The last thing on Borges's mind is the text itself and what it means; what it means is implicit in the managing of it. In "The Library of Babel," we never know what books the librarians are searching for and *why*, rather they're concerned with *how* to locate, extract, and manage preexisting knowledge. Similarly, it's taken for granted that *Quixote* is a classic text and therefore unassailable; instead, the emphasis is on the hermeneutics of how such a perfect replica came into being in the first place. As early as 1941, Borges is proposing that content is no longer king; instead context and reception are the new sites of meaning, an idea that was explored in the theoretically authorless practices of 1960s conceptual art.

There's a Borgesian slant on artist Lawrence Weiner's famous 1969 declaration: "THE ARTIST MAY CONSTRUCT THE WORK / THE WORK MAY BE FABRICATED / THE WORK NEED NOT BE BUILT." There's a Borgesian twist as well in Sol LeWitt's 1966 notion that "in conceptual art the idea or concept is the most important aspect of the work. When an artist uses a conceptual form of art, it means that all of the planning and decisions are made beforehand and the execution is a perfunctory affair." As if to say that if all fictions are, in fact, fiction, then perhaps it's just as good to propose them as to realize them. Borges questions labor and value in a realm where perspiration is plentiful and remuneration is scarce. Why bother? Borges echoes the Parisian radical May '68 sloganeers, when they scrawled across city walls: "NEVER WORK" and "PEOPLE WHO WORK GET BORED WHEN THEY DON'T WORK. PEOPLE WHO DON'T WORK NEVER GET BORED." Perhaps, then, in a Borgesian sense, it's best *not* to write but to propose: propositions are gateways to utopias.

All of this is a far cry from the activism of Aaron Swartz, Chelsea Manning, Julian Assange, and Edward Snowden, where theoretical propositions are not an option. These four individuals enacted Michel Foucault's notion of *parrhesia*—the impulse to speak the truth at whatever cost—and they paid dearly for it: Manning in prison, Snowden in exile, Assange in limbo, and Swartz with his life. And it's here where the distinctions between activism and art, politics and poetry, fact and fiction become clear. I am reminded of Ludwig Wittgenstein's admonition: "Do not forget that a poem, although it is composed in the language of information, it is not used in the language-game of giving information." Such is the freedom and beauty of poetry. Politics, however, is another matter.

CHAPTER 5

Dream Machines and Eternidays

A figure is staring intently at a device cradled in his hands. His shoulders are rounded, his back is hunched, and his head is bowed at the neck. Both elbows are flat against his body, bent at forty-five-degree angles. His fingers are moving about the surface of the device. While the world goes on with its business around him, he is completely oblivious; he can't stop staring at the device. This is a magical device, for it has the ability to transport him to exotic and faraway places: exciting sea adventures, lumbering hippopotamuses wading in rivers, colorful rice fields halfway around the world. The device completely engulfs every inch of his being, when suddenly, in an instant, he raises his head, pauses for a moment, and places the device—a small book—on top of a jumble of other books in a cramped bookstall on the Seine. The camera zooms out, showing us rows of men in the same exact posture, all of them, heads bowed, deeply absorbed in small books they're reading, oblivious to the world around them. These men, in formation, posture, countenance, and absorption bear a striking resemblance to the lines of people I see hunched over their devices on the platform of the West Fourth Street station waiting for their rush hour trains home.

This film, *Bookstalls*, is by Joseph Cornell, the American surrealist, and was cobbled together at his kitchen table on Utopia Parkway in Queens, New York, in the late 1930s. Like most of Cornell's films, he didn't shoot a thing; this silent film was assembled from found footage taken from his vast collection of early cinema reels that he kept in his basement. What Cornell shows us in this film is that dreaming in public is nothing new. Be it books or smartphones, these wondrous devices have the capability of lifting us out of our everyday circumstances and transporting us elsewhere without our ever having to move an inch. Although Cornell rarely traveled—in his lifetime, he never journeyed farther than New England—he was able to span the globe and time travel across centuries through his artworks: films, boxes, assemblages, and collages. Peer into a tiny Cornell box and you'll be magically transported to some other world created entirely from scavenged flotsam and jetsam—old prints, maps, Ping-Pong balls, shattered wineglasses, sand—that Cornell salvaged from his ramblings in junk shops and bookstores, which he then assembled into his famous dream machines.

There's much about Joseph Cornell's life and work that anticipates our digital age. The origins of our computer interfaces and operating systems, with their delicate balance of logic and absurdity, mirror the surrealist aesthetics of Cornell's boxes. The Internet's grassroots ethos of sharing, open source, and free culture were in full swing on Utopia Parkway. His varied artistic output could be called multimedia some seventy-five years before it became the digital norm. An early adapter of indie culture, his living room became a pop-up cinema for like-minded film buffs in the 1930s who had no access to already-forgotten silent classics from the turn of the century. Even after he became world famous, Cornell was a one-man gift economy, giving many of his boxes away to neighborhood children as toys. He was self-educated before it became common. Although he became one of the most famous artists of the twentieth century, he didn't attend art school or have any other formal training. In fact, he never even finished high school, preferring instead to teach himself philosophy, poetry, history, and aesthetics by devouring books from libraries, the way we harvest web-based educational resources from the comfort of our couches. Our relentless management of information—downloading, cataloging, tagging, duplicating, and archiving—was expressed in this early modernist's working and collecting habits. By the time he died, his little house had become his own library—his private Wikipedia—prompting one observer to quip that he was "a kind of curator of culture, and his house on Utopia Parkway a bureau of which he was trustee, director and staff." And, like many Internet fanboys, he was a geeky loner, more comfortable with distant correspondence than he was with face-to-face encounters; although his meatspace social network was wide, he died a virgin.

Born in 1903 into an upper-middle-class family, his father, a traveling salesman, died young, sending Cornell, his handicapped brother, and mother into a downward spiral of poverty. They ended up in a modest working-class house on Utopia Parkway where Cornell spent the rest of his life. Devoted to his mother and acting as a caretaker for his brother, Cornell eked out a living for the family by working a series of low-level jobs during the day and working on his art at night. Due to his familial and financial burdens, he didn't travel much farther than Manhattan—a twenty-minute train ride from his home—so he invented a series of self-sustaining measures that made it possible for him to create and live in a world of his own.

Cornell was a massive collector, verging on hoarder, who stockpiled all types of ephemera and meticulously organized them by arcane but precise systems so that anything could be retrieved at a moment's notice. By the time he died in 1972, his tiny house was jammed with cultural artifacts: three thousand books and magazines, a comparable number of record albums and vintage films, enough diaries and letters to now fill more than thirty reels of microfilm, and tens of thousands of examples of ephemera—from postage stamps to clay pipes, from theatrical handbills to birds' nests. When he wasn't working his job, he was out gathering materials for his boxes, trolling the vast used bookstores of Manhattan's Fourth Avenue, hunting for illustrations that might be incorporated into his work. He became an ardent collector of media—films, in particular—making trips to New Jersey warehouses where Dumpsters' full of reels were being unceremoniously tossed, regarded as artistically worthless, salvageable only for the silver nitrate they contained. In this way, Cornell was able to assemble one of the largest collections of early cinema in America. The steady stream of cinephiles who passed through his house trading films with him in the 1930s hadn't a clue that Cornell was an artist. To them, he was an eccentric homegrown archivist.

He was most famous for his box constructions. Made of wood, they're often no wider than a laptop, and no deeper than a few inches. Often they are divided with wooden slats into multiple compartments. Each compartment contains an element, object, or image: in one section is an image of a bird clipped from a Victorian lithograph, in another is a collection of small seashells, in a third a few strands of ribbon. Depending on the theme of the box, the images tangentially relate to one another. In one box, most of the elements are naturally themed, in another they are celestial, in yet another they are classical. But not always. There are always odd things thrown in—compasses, clay pipes, marbles—that gently disrupt the overarching themes, nudging the box into the realm of dreams.

The same way our devices are launching pads for web voyages, Cornell's boxes are launching pads for interior voyages. Each box has an interface, its own operating and navigational systems through which we may experience it. It's no coincidence that Cornell extensively used maps and globes in his work. From the repeated rows of iconic imagery to the

way the space is divided into small windows, they are struc-
turally reminiscent of the way our desktops are ordered. In a
way, they seem like primitive computers. The names of web
browsers—Navigator, Safari, and Explorer—could equally
be applied to Cornell's boxes.

My desktop resembles a Joseph Cornell box. It's at once
a coherent space and a fractured one. My operating system
unifies everything, but each window has its own agenda,
shattering any real sense of accord. Like Cornell's boxes, I
never have just one window open, I always have many. And
like his compartments, each window represents its own
world. Sometimes those windows contain related content—
right now my Facebook page and Twitter app are showing
much of the same stuff—and other times, they're really disjunctive: in one window is a dull spreadsheet, while another
is streaming a slick music video.

My screen is cluttered with graphic images, from the
icon-festooned dock at the bottom to the pull-down menus
at the top, where various icons show me the time, weather, my battery life, Wi-Fi strength, and so forth. The windows on my screen are piled on top of each other so thickly
that I can only see fragments of each. Yet, there's nothing
confusing about this. Somehow, I understand where everything is and what each window does, even in this chaotic,
cluttered, and shattered environment. And then there are
worlds within worlds. In one of my windows, I'm streaming
CNBC's *Squawk Box*, whose video stream itself is divided
into no fewer than fourteen windows all going at once, each

showing something different. The main window has an image of the three hosts sitting around a table in a studio that itself has dozens of screens, computer monitors, and whose physical stage set is crowded with reflective surfaces. The hosts' window is ringed by more boxes showing various stock charts and numbers; there's a clock, a logo, and a title box. Along the bottom are two crawls, one with news, the other with market numbers, one on top of the other. On the right side of the window are stacked boxes with market numbers and charts. The entire landscape is moving and fluid: new words and numbers continue to appear and just as quickly disappear. A network logo and HD+ symbol reside in the lower-right corner. There's a strong visual connection between both Cornell's boxes and what my computer screen looks like at this very moment. My screen and the many windows contained therein feeling like an M. C. Escher drawing—worlds within worlds within worlds.

Cornell predicted this. Boxes and screens are everywhere, from guys that work on Wall Street literally enveloped in flat-screen monitors to sports bars where every surface is showing a different game. In 1969 Andy Warhol said, "Everybody should have two television sets. So you can watch two at a time. Every time you see the President, he has three." Sometimes I feel like all this distraction is life training for a distracted world—which is not always a bad thing. Running contrary to popular opinion that we're losing our ability to concentrate, the Princeton historian Michael Wood calls distraction another kind of concentration: "The distracted person is not just absent or daydreaming, he/she is attracted, however fitfully, by a rival interest." Wood says that distraction contains certain elements of concentration, but not enough to make it respectable. When we concentrate, we're no longer curious—we're concentrated, after all—foreclosing on surprises that distraction can bring. True, distraction might mean missing the main event. But what if nobody knows anymore what or where the main event is?

Seeing ourselves and our lives reflected in our interfaces is a key part of the reason we stay so attached to them. Cornell thought it was important to include his viewers in his boxes, which is why they often contain mirrors. Glimpse into his boxes and in one or two of his "windows" you'll find an image of yourself. The myth of Narcissus, who mistook his own reflection in the water for another person, underlies the success of social media. The psychologist Jacques Lacan had a name for this, the "mirror stage," which says that when an infant sees him- or herself in a mirror for the first time, there is an immediate identification with that image. Up until that point, the baby has no knowledge of itself as an individual, unified being; instead, wholly dependent on others, it has only a fractured sense of self. From that time on, according to Lacan, the image of oneself as a whole person is intoxicating; we become hooked on external representations of ourselves, which goes a long way toward explaining why we love to find ourselves tagged in Facebook photos or have our tweets retweeted. If the Internet is a giant copying machine, then every time we see ourselves reflected in it, we are more drawn to it. It's no surprise that we can't stop self-googling or try as we might, we can't leave Facebook. There's too much of *us* reflected in it to walk away from.

Interface designers know this well. Each time I open my Twitter feed, I see an image of myself—a flattering one, after all, I chose it—in the navigation bar. And on Facebook, my little avatar shows up next to every comment box at the end of every single thread. Scrolling down my Facebook feed on my computer, I see me—rendered as an icon—repeatedly and endlessly. It's no wonder I feel I have a vested interest in every conversation happening there. Every time I open a social media app, the first thing it shows me is how I am reflected in it: how many times I'm mentioned in comments, how many likes I got, how many retweets and favorites I have amassed. This accumulation is social media's capital, a symbolic currency for which "I" is the metric of valuation.

McLuhan theorized that the insertion of one's self into media was a basic precept of electronic media. Commenting on the myth of Narcissus, he claimed that "this extension of [Narcissus] by mirror numbed his perceptions until he became the servomechanism of his own extended or repeated image. The nymph Echo tried to win his love with fragments of his own speech, but in vain. He was numb. He had adapted to his extension of himself and had become a closed system. Now the point of this myth is the fact that men at once become fascinated by any extension of themselves in any material other than themselves." If there's a better description of the mechanics of social media, I don't know it.

Cornell spent an enormous amount of time drifting around the streets of Manhattan, where he would see his reflection in the glass of shop windows. Like social media, when we see ourselves reflected in a window display, we become entwined—literally overlaid—with what is being sold to us. Shop window displays invoke Renaissance scholar Leon Battista Alberti's dictate that the proportions of the spectator and the display figure should be nearly the same, creating a symbiosis between the consumer and the desired object. In 1435, Alberti wrote a treatise about perspective and painting called *De pictura*. In it, he positioned the human figure as the basis for the division of the canvas into proportional parts. He was among the first to imagine the canvas as being a transparent window on to the world—like a plate of glass—upon which an image could be literally traced, resulting in accurate representations of reality. In doing so, he theorized the idea of perspective: if the canvas was indeed a transparent glass or window, we could look into it toward a vanishing point far in the distance. For Alberti, the canvas/window was a twofold surface that was both opaque (canvas) and transparent (illusionistic).

Alberti's ideas percolated throughout Europe over the centuries. In the 1680s, for instance, when Versailles was built, the vertical casement window—which still reflected

Alberti's human proportion as a standard—was extensively employed, resulting in a national idiom called the French window. This type of window remained the standard in classical French architecture for the next 250 years until the early 1920s when Le Corbusier introduced the horizontal window, a concept that was widely attacked as being unpatriotic. Le Corbusier, of course, was part of modernism's thrust toward "flatness," which reached its zenith in the 1950s when Clement Greenberg insisted that the surface of a painting was not a space of depiction for anything other than the act of painting itself. His hard-core anti-illusionism was exemplified by the abstract expressionists, for whom flatness was the gospel.

As consumer technology evolved, it also adopted an ethos of flatness. Similar to modernism, it strived to strip away vestiges of cumbersome apparatuses. When televisions first appeared, they were encased in wood, posing as pieces of furniture, an attempt to seamlessly integrate the cold, mechanical technology into cozy domestic environments. By the 1970s, led by the smart design of Sony's Trinitron, TV sets were freed from their furniture function, and like modernist painting, were able to become what they were, leading the way for today's floating flat screens and plasmas. Similarly, each subsequent release of smartphones and tablets is thinner. Yet contradictorily, there is a drive to render believably illusionistic depths of field on these flat surfaces: video games and virtual reality interfaces seek to literally move you through "worlds" in hyperdimensional detail.

It's been said that as interface design has progressed, it's grown more childlike with each passing iteration. The first computers were unquestionably made for adults. Their command lines required you to know how to read and how to type. But with the introduction of graphical user interfaces, operating systems migrated to large and overly simple iconic representations of complex phenomena—so simple that children could operate them. When interfaces were strictly linguistic, their languages tended to be logical, with a one-to-one correspondence between command and functionality: the "ls" command in Unix or "dir" in DOS listed your directories—and that's all it did. But once GUIs appeared, the visually expressed commands became interpretative and vague. Every icon set is drawn by a graphic artist and is therefore interpretative, with each operating system attempting to visually distinguish itself from the others: think of Windows' recycling bin as opposed to Mac's trash can. But neither is accurate: computer documents are neither permanently deleted nor recycled. In truth, they are partially overwritten.

The idea that the content of any medium is always another medium is expressed in the metaphor of the desktop. From the very beginning of GUIs—screen interfaces displaying icons and folders, etc. which mask the lines of code that actually run your computer—it's as if the entire contents of a mid-twentieth-century office had been dumped on your computer. There are stacks of "paper" you can click on, "notepads" you can write on, "folders" where you can store your "documents," "calculators" that have "buttons" you can "push." To this day, I still edit my documents in the program "Office" while browsing web "pages." (I often ask myself what exactly constitutes a web page. I still haven't found the answer.) The office DNA is so embedded in our computing operating systems that even our mobile devices, bereft of desktops, still bear its predigital iconography. On my iPhone, my Notes app depicts a square legal pad, my camera icon looks like a 1950s Nikon, my Mail app is a standard number 10 white envelope, and my Phone app shows an outline of a mid-twentieth-century telephone receiver.

Early graphical icons were flat, nondimensional representations. A folder—based on a classic manila folder—was a simply drawn outline of a tabbed folder. With successive iterations folders became dimensional, modeled with drop shadows. Later on, when you'd click on that 3-D folder, it would animate, literally opening itself up to show its paper contents before spinning off into a new window. (And now, on Apple products at least, everything's flattened back out again in the latest OS.) While these animations and heavy graphics slowed systems down, they also opened up the role of the interface and graphic designer to inject playful surrealist elements into the once-dry textual environment. It's hard to imagine an interface designer not wanting to reference Dalí's melting watches when creating desktop icons (even the clock icon on my iPhone is depicted by a clock with hands). The title of his famous painting *The Persistence of Memory* has echoes of RAM (temporary data, such as files that can be easily deleted, altered, or overwritten) and ROM (permanent data, such as your operating system, that can't be easily deleted, altered, or overwritten), the foundation of our computers. About his painting Dalí wrote: "I am the first to be surprised and often terrified by the images I see appear upon my canvas. I register without choice and with all possible exactitude the dictates of my subconscious, my dreams." Substitute the words "upon my canvas" for "in my browser," and it becomes clear how surrealism and its ethos are hardwired into the very core of our computing experience.

Floating in the middle of my screen is a series of vertical blocky gray images, one atop another, on a jet-black background: a birdhouse with two holes in it, a bell that tilts to the right, an envelope that has the stem of a speech bubble protruding from its bottom-left corner, a series of three vertical dots next to a series of three vertical lines, a head without a neck, and a magnifying glass tilted to the left. All are the same size and all are rendered in the identical style. Like a rebus, I could assemble them into some sort of a narrative or simply enjoy their playful visuality, their randomness, their absurdity. They hang in the space of my screen the way a moon and stars poetically dangle in a Joan Miró painting or how vaguely abstract figures hauntingly populate a desolate Yves Tanguy landscape. But there's very little that's artistic or poetic about it; it's a description of the navigation bar on my Twitter app.

The icons in the dock that runs along the bottom of my

screen are equally surreal. If I turn on the magnification function and enlarge them, I'm surprised at what I find. Several times a day I use my Preview app to view PDFs and images.* As an icon no larger than a cufflink, nestled in my dock with all my other icons, I think of it as "the blue one with a few lines through it." I click on it, it does its job, and I never think about it again. But if I scale it up, a bizarre and rather incomprehensible series of images reveals itself. The icon consists of two photographs printed on "paper" with a white border, each skewed, laid atop one another. The photo on the bottom appears to be a picture of an old yellow stone wall and the photo on top, the most prominent image, is of a child standing on a beach, framed by a crisp blue sky. As the waves crash behind him, he's got his hands clasped in what could be interpreted as a quasi-religious salutation, the kind of thing you always see the Dalai Lama doing. He's got a sort of beatific half smile and his hair, in cowlicks, is soaked as if he just got out of the water. He's clothed in a gray garment that is open at the chest, which could either be a raincoat (why would anyone wear a raincoat on the beach on a sunny day?) or a drenched gray karate *gi* (a gi is a strange choice for a beachwear). On top of the photos sits a magnifying loupe, the type used to examine

---

* This Preview icon came with the Mac Mavericks OS. In the next OS, Yosemite, the child was removed and the magnifying lens was replaced with what looks like a 35 mm camera lens. In terms of narrative and choices, it still makes very little sense. There has been much online speculation about who "preview kid" actually is and why he is there but no one seems to have come up with an answer.

photographs or media spreads while editing them. It strikes me as odd that the imagery in this icon refers to dead media: printed photographs and a loupe. After all, Preview examines only digital imagery and if you wanted to zoom in on what you're looking at, you'd click a button, not gaze through a lens. A similar nostalgia permeates contemporary art as well. "Today, no exhibition is complete without some form of bulky, obsolete technology," observes the art historian Claire Bishop. "The gently clunking carousel of a slide projector or the whirring of an 8-mm or 16-mm film reel . . . Today, film's soft warmth feels intimate compared with the cold, hard digital image, with its excess of visual information (each still contains far more detail than the human eye could ever need)."

While these Preview app images tell a certain story, they also refuse to tell a story, a textbook example of the nineteenth-century poet Comte de Lautréamont's definition of surrealistic absurdity: "a sewing machine and an umbrella on a dissection table." Like a Cornell box, they're *suggestive*: of place, ethos, nature, environment, corporate values, positivism, world peace, and religion, while deftly avoiding taking an explicit position on any one of them. The icon is *evocative*, not *narrative*; and its style of evocation is grounded in the disjunctive surrealist tradition. The icon gives two conflicting messages: functionality (it reads documents really well) and non sequitur (I can't figure out why these images represent a functional program). They're not really in conflict with one another—

they seem to work quite well together, if bizarrely—but it points to the fact that underlying the strict surface "logic" of our operating systems is a subconscious irrationality or sentimentality.

Your computer's ROM is the basement, attic, or toolshed of your computer, where stuff goes into deep storage. Cornell's house was one big hard drive, particularly his basement, where he stored his vast collection of ephemera, much of which went into making his boxes. Down in the basement was also where he kept dossiers stuffed with scads of flotsam and jetsam on various starlets like Greta Garbo and Hedy Lamarr, with whom he was obsessed. When he attended film premieres or spent evenings at the ballet, he'd return home to his basement media collection to pore over his archived images of the stars he'd seen, ultimately incorporating their images into his boxes.

Joseph Cornell was the ultimate fanboy. In the mid-1950s, for instance, Cornell became obsessed with Allegra Kent, a gorgeous young ballerina he had read about in *Newsweek*. Finally, he got the courage up to meet her by writing and asking her to appear in one of his films. She agreed to see him at her home in Manhattan, but the meeting didn't go well. "He was terribly thin, a strange, gaunt, intense-looking creature," Kent recalled. "I noticed his hands which were discolored from perhaps shellac or varnish. I immediately sensed that he really liked me, which was a little scary. Fans can be crazy. You don't know what to expect from a fan." On the spot, Kent told him that she wasn't interested in appearing in his film and sent him on his way.

Cornell's crushes remind me of Internet fanboy culture, in particular, of Harry Knowles, the founder of the influential website Ain't It Cool News, a vast repository of geek culture, comics, as well as information on sci-fi, fantasy, horror and action movies and TV shows. Like Cornell, Knowles built his site from his bedroom, where in 1994 he started posting to newsgroups, swapping rumors about upcoming films. He ended up writing film reviews on the newsgroups, which formed the basis for his website, which he launched in 1996. Quickly, the site drew hundreds of collaborators, many of whom leaked scandalous insider information about Hollywood—rumors, secret film scripts, advance screening reviews—much to the chagrin of the Hollywood studios, who up until that time were able to keep a tight rein on the publicity surrounding films before they were released.

A 1997 *New York Times* profile on Knowles sounds like it could almost be describing Cornell: "Harry Jay Knowles is sprawled on the edge of his bed, clicking at the keyboard of his Packard Bell computer. It's 10 A.M., and he is just starting his day in a tiny airless room crammed with videos, unread film scripts, movie posters ("Bride of Frankenstein," "King Kong," etc.) and 8-by-10 glossies of Marilyn Monroe, Britt Ekland, Ray Milland and the original Superman, Kirk Alyn.

A grinning Vincent Price shrunken head lies in a box on the floor." Knowles's parents ran a movie memorabilia shop in Austin, Texas, where he grew up, that was crammed with pulp fiction, fanzines, and comics. They would set up shop on weekends at comics conventions and film festivals. "I was their experiment," Knowles said in an interview. "They unleashed everything on me. I saw porn, all the Universal monster movies, all the Charlie Chan films, all the Sherlock Holmes things, all the Fred and Ginger movies. Film for me became how I related to everything else." Like Cornell toiling in his cramped basement, Knowles created his empire from the confines of his bedroom, at the helm of a vast correspondence network that was done mostly from afar.

A 2012 pilot for a YouTube show, *Ain't It Cool with Harry Knowles*, is shot in his father's Austin, Texas, basement (these guys love basements) and features Knowles—a heavyset man in a loud Hawaiian shirt, goatee, and chunky black-framed glasses—seated behind a desk talking to a camera, surrounded by piles of ephemera. Aping the style of *Pee-wee's Playhouse*, Knowles shows old movie clips, opens a mailbox where he finds a catalog for a Captain America auction filled with props for sale, converses about comics with an animated cardboard boiler, and browses through a leaked film script. Information flies at him from all directions, all without him ever having to leave his chair. It's a meatspace enactment of the vaporous networks that made Knowles famous, while forwarding Cornell's methodology into the heart of the digital age—accumulating and organizing vast amounts of information, not into the art economy of boxes, but into websites, hits, and likes.

As "free culture" geeks, both Cornell and Knowles share an elastic sense of copyright. In Knowles's case, he leaked once-private information, posting documents in full. Cornell, too, subscribed to the idea of "borrower's rights," or, as his friend the poet Mina Loy put it, "A contemporary brain wielding a prior brain is a more potent implement than a paintbrush." Stuck in Queens, Cornell never got to go to Paris or Florence to see the masterpieces he loved so much. Instead, he surrounded himself with reproductions of them, which came to stand in for the originals, similar to how our crummy AVI rips become more beloved than the "real" 35-millimeter version of a film that we'll probably never see in a theater. In the early twentieth century, the networks that fed Cornell's proclivities were the United States Postal Service; his exposure to much of the world's great art came to him through printed reproductions in books and magazines. When he wished to incorporate an image into one of his boxes, he would photostat it, preserving the original in his archive. To him, the copy was a natural thing, more real than the original. While remix culture is commonplace today, it was much rarer when Cornell began his artistic life. He had one rule about his art—that no element in it could be original. Everything he used had to be found or reproduced.

Cornell might've been the only filmmaker in the history of film who never learned to operate a camera. Instead, his early films, like *Bookstalls*, were all recomposed from found footage.* His 1936 film *Rose Hobart* is an ancestor of the Internet supercut—those fast-paced montages that compile, say, every swear word uttered in *Deadwood* or every scene in *Talladega Nights* in which the phrase "shake and bake" is roared with an accompanying fist bump. To make *Rose Hobart*, Cornell took a trashy grade-B jungle flick and, with scissors and Scotch tape, cut it up and put it back together out of order. The clichéd story line was happily disposed of and in its place appeared a series of disconnected fantasy sequences. When Cornell screened it, he projected it through a pane of deep-blue glass, imparting a dreamlike quality to it. The film was accompanied by a campy soundtrack from warbly 78 rpm discs that Cornell would hand crank.

Rose Hobart was an influential film that spawned genres of "cut up" films, the best known of which is Christian Marclay's *The Clock* (2010), a twenty-four-hour film that is literally a clock, displaying in real time the passing minutes of a day. Comprised of thousands of recycled film clips, *The Clock* is an epic work of montage. To create it, Marclay and his assistants watched thousands of DVDs and extracted scenes that had clocks somewhere in them. They collected them until every minute of the day was accounted for, then strung them together chronologically. Narrative, genre, or style were of no concern; the only thing that mattered was the presence of a clock in the shot. These scenes were edited

---

* Only later in his career, when he wanted to generate original footage, Cornell would hire young filmmakers like Larry Jordan or Stan Brakhage as cameramen to shoot it for him.

down to exactly one-minute lengths and synced to real time so that if you, for example, entered the theater at 4:34 P.M. and looked up at the screen, the clock in the background of the film at that moment would read 4:34. Walk into the cinema at noon, a clock would read 12:00; the following minute the clip changed and another clock would show 12:01. The entire project was mellifluously sequenced by Marclay, so that one scene seamlessly melded into another, binding the entire enterprise into a smooth, sensual, and riveting experience. In one way, it's a giant work of montage; in another, it's actually a clock that tells the correct time.

Befittingly, the film has been widely celebrated and crowds around the globe continue to this day to queue up to view the piece in person. Critical praise has been superlatively lavish: the art critic Roberta Smith called *The Clock* the "ultimate work of appropriation art." What's more, *The Clock* manages to bridge the art world with popular culture, which might account, in part, for its popularity. While Marclay contemplated crowdsourcing the project on the web, he felt that the supercut's jagged and rough editing style would be at odds with the seamless quality he was after.

So far, so good: a massively popular work constructed in the style of broad-based web trends, which is also acclaimed, valorized, funded, exhibited, and collected by the most powerful art world institutions. And yet, the elephant in the room is copyright: few have mentioned that Marclay hasn't cleared any permissions with Hollywood for his work. Marclay explained his idea of copyright in an interview with the

New Yorker: "If you make something good and interesting and not ridiculing someone or being offensive, the creators of the original material will like it." It's something he's stood by for the past three decades, weaving a career out of sampling, appropriation, remixing, and plunderphonics; clearly, for Marclay, it appears to be working.

Yet there seems to be a schism between popular culture and the museum. While Marclay's actions are hailed, media policing agencies like the MPAA (Motion Picture Association of America) and RIAA (Recording Industry Association of America) have been waging an ongoing campaign against file sharers who create remixes out of copyrighted material not unlike what Marclay does. *The Clock* is a product of the digital age—it's hard to imagine it being constructed out of celluloid—but, for a work borne of preexisting material and exuding free culture frisson, *The Clock* is tightly controlled: a full-length version can't be found on YouTube or on the Pirate Bay. Instead, like a conventional market-based work of art, there is only an expensive, limited edition available to a select few institutions that can afford its half-million-dollar price tag. More so, at a time when much cultural power is based on multiplicity, nongeographical specificity, and wide dissemination, *The Clock* can only be viewed during special times under pristine conditions—often for a steep museum admission price—which sends mixed signals to the Internet-savvy public. Although the work is predicated on a complex computer program that syncs the film with the actual time in any given location, one assumes that a web version that does the same thing wouldn't be too hard to create, a move that would satisfy both worlds.

Time is an obsession that both Marclay and Cornell share. There's something both temporal and atemporal about *The Clock*: it tells the exact time of day, but as an artwork it has no expiration date. Since it's comprised of used and mostly classic materials, the work has a timeless feel, riding an edge between the momentary and the eternal. Furthermore, its site specificity ensures that it's always current: when it shows at noon, there are usually big crowds in the theater, but at 4:00 A.M.—if the museum is open—just a few diehard fans are scattered about. Those quiet moments in the middle of the night belonged to Cornell, who was an insomniac. To him, every day was—as he called it—an *eterniday*. He came up with this idea by working all day at a crummy job, and then coming home to take care of his mother and brother. Then, when the house quieted down, he would stay up all night doing his work in a sleep-deprived dream state—a state between states—half-asleep, half-awake. Like his antecedents the sleeping surrealist poets, he came to prefer being in that twilight zone and later, when he was able to quit his job, would nap sporadically throughout the day so that he could work all night.

Cornell was 24/7 before we were 24/7. When I address a global audience late at night on social media, I am acutely aware that the people I am addressing may be on the other side of the world, wide awake in the middle of their day. I sometimes tailor the content of my posts to appeal directly to that audience across the planet, forsaking my local community because I assume them to be sleeping. The digital age has ushered in atemporality; the hum of the computer and the grinding of the network exists outside of subjective, personal, local, traditional, and even communitarian, traditions of time, a condition explored in Jonathan Crary's book *24/7: Late Capitalism and the Ends of Sleep*. Crary gives a Cornellian example of where labor, technology, sleeplessness, and the cosmos meet. He tells of an effort in the 1990s by a space consortium to build and launch satellites to reflect sunlight back on the earth with the intention of creating, literally, an *eterniday*. (The company's slogan was "Daylight all night long.") Outfitted with paper-thin reflective material two hundred meters in diameter, it would have the capacity to illuminate a ten-mile-square area of the earth in the middle of the night. Originally intended so that miners working in Siberia would have more "daylight" hours under which to toil, it was quickly embraced as a way of extending office hours in cities. There were protests, however, from groups who argued that the night sky was "a commons to which all humanity is entitled to have access, and the ability to experience the darkness of night and observe the stars is a basic human right that no corporation can nullify." The project was killed, but that didn't stop us, our machines, and our networks from working *eternidays*.

In the winter of 1955 through 1956, Cornell held an exhibition of boxes in a New York City gallery entitled *Winter Night Skies*, which incorporated star charts of constellations.

The series was stark: white boxes with deep-blue images of night skies, framed in architecture he called Hôtel de l'Etoile. Joseph Cornell loved the winter stars at night. Gazing out his kitchen window at 4:00 A.M. at the bright stars embedded in the pitch-black sky over a silent Queens, half-asleep, half-awake, he was an armchair voyager traveling the cosmos basking in—as he called it—"light from other days."

CHAPTER 6

I Shoot Therefore I Am

Like Joseph Cornell's basement, my many hard drives are packed with downloaded books, movies, images, and music. While I spend a lot of time downloading them, copying them, renaming them, and organizing them into their respective folders, once they're neatly filed away, I tend to forget about them. Rummaging through them, I'm often surprised at what I find, as was the case when I was recently in the mood to listen to the music of the American midcentury composer Morton Feldman. I dug in to my MP3 drive, found my Feldman folder, and opened it up. Among the various folders in the directory was one labeled the Complete Works of Morton Feldman. I was surprised to see it there; I didn't remember downloading it. Curious, I looked at its date—2009—and realized that I must've grabbed it during the heyday of MP3 sharity blogs. I opened it to find seventy-nine albums as zipped files. I unzipped three of them, listened to part of one, closed the folder, and haven't opened it since. In the digital ecosystem, the apparatuses surrounding the cultural artifacts are often more engaging than the artifacts themselves. In an unanticipated twist to John Perry Barlow's 1994 prediction that in the digital age we'd be able to enjoy wine without the bottles, we've now come to prefer the bottles to the wine.

Back in 1983, the media critic and philosopher Vilém Flusser (1920–1991) described this exact phenomenon in a little book called *Towards a Philosophy of Photography*. Flusser claimed that the content of any given photograph is actually the camera that produced it. He continued with a series of nested apparatuses: the content of the camera is the programming that makes it function; the content of the programming is the photographic industry that produces it; and the content of the photographic industry is the military-industrial complex in which it is situated, and so forth. He viewed photography from a completely technical standpoint. In Flusser's view, the traditional content of the cultural artifact is completely subsumed by the apparatuses—technical, political, social, and industrial—surrounding, and thereby defining, it.

Although he was writing about analog, print-based photography, Flusser's ideas go a long way to explain our changing relationship to the cultural artifact in the digital age, reminding us of Moholy-Nagy's prediction that "those who are ignorant in matters of photography will be the illiterates of tomorrow."

The mistake most make in reading Flusser is to assume he's talking about analog photography. Yes, he is, but that's the least relevant part. Imagine, instead, that everything he's saying about photography he's saying about the digital. This requires an act of imaginative translation on our part, but once you make that leap, you realize that this 1983 text astonishingly directly addresses our situation some three and a half decades later. For instance, Flusser claimed that the camera was the ancestor of apparatuses that are in the process of "robotizing all aspects of our lives, from one's most public acts to one's innermost thoughts, feelings, and desires." And when we look at social media—from blogs, to Twitter, to Facebook, and to Instagram—we can see he was correct. Like the camera, the Twitter apparatus coerces us, seducing us to tweet, and we dutifully obey. Once we're hooked in to the game, we become compulsive: the more we tweet, the more we enrich the program, thereby increasing its standing within the larger social media apparatus and ultimately boosting Twitter's share price. In Flusserian terms, it doesn't really matter what we tweet (content); it just matters that we keep tweeting (apparatus). For Flusser, the content of any medium is always the series of apparatuses that produced it.

In fact, content plays little role in Flusser's writing. A photograph is not a carrier of memories—your baby pictures are interchangeable with a million other baby pictures—but a predetermined artifact spit out by the camera apparatus. The camera is a voracious, greedy device, programmed to stalk images the way an animal stalks prey: the camera smells blood and (literally) snaps. On Instagram, the more you shoot, the more you become addicted to the photographic apparatus, which Flusser likens to opium addiction or being on a "photograph-trip." In the end, you wind up working for the camera and the industry that produced it. The more people who use an apparatus, the more feedback the company receives about its camera, the smarter it becomes, and the more users it draws to its base, thereby increasing the manufacturer's bottom line. For this reason, Instagram keeps adding new filter sets and features in order to retain and broaden its users. To Instagram, what people are photographing is beside the point; the real point is that they keep posting.

Photography is easy. Anyone can push a button and produce a good photograph without having a clue as to the inner workings of a camera. A recent Apple ad underscores this: "Every day, millions of amazing photos and videos are shot with iPhone. That's because the iPhone makes it easy—for everyone—to shoot amazing photos and video." If taking good photos were difficult—once upon a time it took a great deal of mastery to take a good photograph (f-stops, light meters, shutter speeds)—Instagram would never be as popular as it is today. The programmers of cameras also strive to keep their interfaces as simple as possible, to discourage experimentation outside of its parameters. The simple interface keeps the photographer pushing the button so they can produce, in Flusser's words, "more and more redundant images." The free cost of digital photography keeps the photographer playing the photographic game. (How many people snapping photos with a smartphone only take one shot of any given scene?) Those photos are uploaded to the cloud, where ever-more-redundant photos are stored. Your photo of the Eiffel Tower on Flickr is identically redundant to the millions already stored on Flickr, yet you keep on snapping them (just as I keep downloading MP3s).

I shoot therefore I am. The camera doesn't work for us. We work for the camera. Our compulsive behavior leaves no scene undocumented. When we take a holiday to a foreign country, the photos don't show the sights we saw, they show us the places where the camera has been and what it's done there. We think we're documenting our own memories, but what we're actually producing is memories for the apparatus. The digital photograph's metadata—geotagging, likes, shares, user connectivity, and so forth—proves much more valuable to Instagram than any subject matter it captures. The image is irrelevant in comparison to the apparatuses surrounding it.

Once we buy into a specific apparatus, it's awfully hard to leave it. Your cultural artifact is locked within that system, constrained by its programming. Notice how an Instagram photo can't be resized, e-mailed, or downloaded to your hard drive. It can't exist within any ecosystem other than Instagram's. Notice how easily Instagram can be integrated into the interface of its parent company, Facebook, but how difficult it is to share on Twitter, a competitor's platform. While we play the Instagram game by liking and reposting photos, the apparatus knows otherwise: a like is a way for the shareholder to verify that there are consumers populating the program; the greater and more verifiable the user base, the more valuable the apparatus.

Unless the market determines otherwise, the physical value of most printed photographs are negligible: they're just pieces of paper with information on them—cheap, ubiquitous, unstable, and infinitely reproducible. As opposed to paintings, where the value of the objects resides in their singularity, the value of photographs lies in the information on their surface. Their surface is ephemeral and, in the digital age, rewritable. The photograph is a pivotal artifact, bridging the industrial and postindustrial, embodying the transition from the physical to the purely informational. How that information is distributed determines much of its meaning.

When an image was printed on paper, its ubiquity in physical space was its distributive metric. But even then, the content in a poster or handbill was somewhere other than its image. Flusser writes, "The poster is without value; nobody owns it, it flaps torn in the wind yet the power of the advertising agency remains undiminished . . ." Depending on context and distribution, an image printed on paper could take on different meanings. Unlike, say, an image displayed on a TV screen, a photograph published in a newspaper could be clipped, stuffed into an envelope, and sent to a friend. Passed hand to hand, the movable photographic artifact anticipated our image-sharing networks.

The camera resembles a game of chess. It contains what appears to be an infinite number of possibilities, but in the end those possibilities are prescribed by its programming. Just as every possible move and permutation of a chess game has long been exhausted, every program of the camera too has long been exhausted. In the case of Instagram, with a user base approaching half a million users, its programs are instantly exhausted, resulting in updates that include new features in order to retain users. Although finite, the apparatus must always give the illusion of infinity in order to make each user feel they can never exhaust the program. Or as Flusser says, "Photographs permanently displacing one another according to a program are redundant precisely because they are always 'new' . . ." Your cell phone still makes calls, but you'd be foolish to think that it is about being a telephone in the same way you'd be foolish to think Instagram is about expressive photography. But criticize Instagram, says Flusser, and that critique becomes absorbed in its apparatus: "A number of human beings are struggling against this automatic programming . . . attempting to create a space for human intention in a world dominated by apparatuses. However, the apparatuses themselves automatically assimilate these attempts at liberation and enrich their programs with them."

The only hope? Those who attempt to break the system by doing something with the camera that was never intended by industry: taking intentionally boring photos (Instagram is full of boring photos, but how many of them are made to be intentionally boring?) or blurring images beyond recognition. Twitter is trickier to break. Attempts at self-reflexive critique within the Twitter apparatus are instantly absorbed by the apparatus and celebrated by the corporation to highlight the diversity and playfulness of its expanded user base (once again making the company a more valuable entity).

Flusser's forays into media have framed, theorized, and

unpacked the new complexities of our digital world. By empirically questioning received knowledge and recasting it within crisp lines of history and logic, he's made the digital legible in a time when its theorization is occluded and murky to say the least. When Willem de Kooning said, "The past does not influence me. I influence it," I am reminded of Flusser and how prescient his twentieth-century investigations proved to be for our digitally-soaked twenty-first.

A precursor to Flusser's ideas about apparatus was the Soviet avant-garde filmmaker Dziga Vertov's 1924 concept of the Kino-Eye. Vertov's argument revolves around the idea that the camera's eye has a neutrality that the unaided human eye lacks. It's the difference between you walking down a city street and you looking at an image of that same city street. The image can be contemplated in ways that your eye on the street can't. On the street, the hyperactive and restless human eye is connected to an equally active brain, one that is instructed to see and process images in very specific ways, whereas the camera lens—a superhuman eye—is connected to a machine, one that records with cool precision what it is programmed to capture. Like Flusser's apparatus, Kino-Eye democratizes every image it sees—one image is as good as another—cataloging a visually chaotic world by transforming it into information and creating a stockpile of images for later use, exactly what Google Street View does today. On a darker note, Kino-Eye predicted the rise of the surveillance camera, which restlessly and indiscriminately devours all that passes before its lens. London's ring of steel is Kino-Eye at its most dystopian.

In 1971, the conceptual artist Douglas Huebler set out to make a pre-Internet work of art based on Kino-Eye. His proposition, a cross between sociology and visual art, read: "Throughout the remainder of the artist's lifetime he will photographically document, to the extent of his capacity, the existence of everyone alive in order to produce the most authentic and inclusive representation of the human species that may be assembled in that manner." Understanding the futility of the project—naturally, it remained incomplete at the time of his death—Huebler attempted it anyway, roaming the streets of cities around the world with a film-loaded camera, photographing random passersby. He shot the multitudes from the roofs of buildings and rephotographed pictures of crowds from the day's newspaper. On the web, absurdly totalizing projects like Huebler's are common: one could imagine crowdsourcing digital photos of "everyone alive" on a Tumblr, yet oddly enough, it hasn't yet happened.

The photographer Penelope Umbrico creates huge photo sets from preexisting images she finds on the web. In 2006, she began an ongoing series of collecting images of sunsets posted to Flickr, where she crops out everything but the image of the sun itself, prints them out as 4x6 prints, and arranges them in galleries in massive grids. The variety and subtlety of images are stunning. What could be more banal and clichéd than an image of a sunset? Yet Umbrico's suns are all completely different: some are purplish, some are blue, and others are green. Some suns are tiny dots and others fill the picture frame entirely. Some have halos around them, while others are poetically obscured by wispy clouds. In many, the lens pointed at a bright object creates dramatic solar flares, making them look more like meteorites than suns. A search on Flickr for "sunset" reveals that there are more than twelve million of them housed there, a fact that isn't lost on Umbrico. Echoing Flusser, she states:

> *Perhaps part of the beauty of taking a picture of a sunset is that while you are doing it it's likely that a million other people are doing it as well—at exactly the same time . . . While the intent of photographing a sunset may be to capture something ephemeral or to assert an individual subjective point of view—the result is quite the opposite—through the technology of our common cameras we experience the power of millions of synoptic views, all shared the same way, at the same moment. To claim individual authorship while photographing a sunset is to disengage from this collective practice and therefore negate a large part of why capturing a sunset is so irresistible in the first place.*

The artist Eric Oglander has an ongoing Tumblr called Craigslistmirrors, which features only images of mirrors that are for sale. On first glance, it's a bit perplexing why he'd

want to post a bunch of banal, crappy snapshots of mostly
ugly mirrors, but it quickly becomes clear that folks selling
their mirrors haven't always stopped to consider what those
mirrors are reflecting. Some reflect vast landscapes and clear
blue skies; others reflect curious pets and, in many, the photographers themselves unwittingly appear, oftentimes in
various states of undress. "Either the photographer is going
to be reflected in the mirror or the inside of their home will
be," says Oglander. "It's like an invasion of privacy almost,
and I think that's why people bring the mirrors outside."

Oglander's work references the seminal 1960s mirror
constructions by artist Robert Smithson, which he called
displacements. Robert Smithson didn't make paintings
of the sky; instead, by simply placing a mirror in a grassy
field faceup, Smithson literally displaced an image of the
sky, dropping a square of blue into a sea of green. Blazing
azure one day, smoggy grayish-yellow the next, Smithson's
gestures were at once formal color studies, quiet mediations
on nature, and political statements on ecology. The mirror
is a displacement machine that appropriates all that passes before it. A preprogrammed automaton, the mirror employs no judgment or morals; it indiscriminately displays all
in the most democratic manner possible. The mirror works
around the clock, reflecting a dark room all night long when
its inhabitants are sleeping, or an empty apartment all day
long when its inhabitants are at work. Like its cousin the
surveillance camera, the mirror displays scads of dark data,
but unlike the CCTV, the mirror has no memory: every

image passing across its surface is ephemeral. Great crimes are committed before mirrors; no one is ever the wiser. The mirror, then, is closer to a movie screen than CCTV, a surface upon which images are projected—and then reflected in reverse. Like the CCTV camera, the mirror never goes dark. Smash the mirror; disperse the image. Toss the pieces in the trash; they continue to dumbly reflect.

Since 1996, a group of actors/activists called the Surveillance Camera Players have been staging subversive plays adapted from books such as George Orwell's *1984* and Wilhelm Reich's *The Mass Psychology of Fascism* in front of CCTV cameras. While it's not known if anyone is watching them, their performances—often interrupted by the police—are exhaustively documented by their own cameras in addition to being documented by the surveillance cameras. The Players' message is a political one: "We protest against the use of surveillance cameras in public places because the cameras violate our constitutionally protected right to privacy. We manifest our opposition by performing specially adapted plays directly in front of these cameras . . . Down with Big Brother!"

The cars festooned with cameras that capture Google Street View drive around the world sucking up images. Meant to provide panoramic views of neighborhoods and buildings to accompany their maps, the cameras often capture unexpected and bizarre occurrences, such as women giving birth on the sides of roads, drug deals in progress, or tigers caught prowling suburban parking lots. One artist,

Mishka Henner, scoured online forums where people share the whereabouts of sex workers. He then put those map coordinates into Street View, and indeed, on some of those corners, found images of scantily clad women standing by the sides of the road in isolated areas. He collected these images as a series of photographs that he calls *No Man's Land*. While one might presume these women are sex workers, there's no definite evidence to support that claim. Instead, it's a mix of conjecture culled from the forums with the visual evidence compiled from Street View that gives the story credibility, one that could easily be misconstrued by legal authorities to arrest these women on charges of prostitution. Henner's project underlines the Promethean social and political circumstances that arise when nearly every inch of the planet has been surveyed and posted online and acts as a warning for its potential abuses.

Other artists stage performances for the Street View car as it drives through their neighborhoods. Ben Kinsley and Robin Hewlett have staged seventeenth-century sword fights, hired marching bands, and dressed people up in giant chicken costumes, all for the sake of creating strange images that will be incorporated into Google's official map culture. One online video shows a Street View car approaching on a narrow, rain-slicked Pittsburgh street. The car is forced to drive through a parade with brass bands and baton-spinning majorettes. As the car approaches the parade, it is showered with confetti. Leaving the parade, the car encounters a group of absurdly dressed joggers who animatedly approach it from the opposite direction. Undeterred, the car drives through the spectacle, continuing its recording, seemingly oblivious to the exotic circumstances. Until the car passes this street again, those staged happenings will be preserved on the Google Street View record.

The first popular photoshopped image was of a dark-haired topless woman in white bikini bottoms sitting on a sandy beach in a tropical paradise with her back to the camera. Her name was Jennifer and on that day in 1987 she was photographed gazing out on a picture-perfect landscape, replete with pale turquoise water and a lush tropical island floating to her left on the horizon line. Puffs of clouds hang in a blazing azure sky. This photo came to be known as "Jennifer in Paradise," and was taken by a software developer named John Knoll of his fiancée while they were on vacation in Bora Bora. Shortly afterward, Knoll went on to create Photoshop and this image was distributed with early versions of the program. For many people using Photoshop, Jennifer in Paradise was the first digital image they ever manipulated.

Jennifer's inclusion in Photoshop was casual, even serendipitous. When the demo package was coming together and sample images were needed to digitize, Knoll just grabbed the nearest photo at hand—a 4x6 photograph on paper that happened to be his fiancée in Bora Bora—and tossed it on a scanner. Spontaneously and unwittingly, an icon was born. An online video from 2010 shows Knoll reenacting the Photoshop demonstrations he used to give in order to show the power of his photo-editing suite. Knoll fires up an ancient Mac and pulls up the image of Jennifer. He runs some primitive functions on Jennifer: first he clones her; then he copies, resizes, and pastes a duplicate image of the island and drops it on the horizon. It's kind of creepy: you're watching a reenactment of the future of the image unfurl before your eyes at the site of its inception. And he's not cloning just anything: he's cloning his topless wife, who would be cloned endlessly by the first generation of geeks to get their hands on Photoshop.

Constant Dullaart is an Internet artist who has mounted exhibitions based on the photograph. "Given its cultural significance just from an anthropological point of view I thought it would be interesting to examine what values the image contains," he says. "The fact that it's a white lady, topless, anonymous, facing away from the camera. [Knoll] offers her, objectifying her, in his creation for the reproduction of reality." Dullaart suggests that the negative of that photo should be given to the Smithsonian, to celebrate the time when "the world was young, as it still naïvely believed in the authenticity of the photograph."

As late as 1973 Susan Sontag could still state: "A fake painting (one whose attribution is false) falsifies the history of art. A fake photograph (one which has been retouched or tampered with, or whose caption is false) falsifies reality."

A decade later, Samuel Beckett said the same thing for literature, regarding Duchamp's readymades: "A writer could not do that." Thirty or forty years ago, fakeness was still the exception, not the rule that it is in today's digital world. The binary of true/false art/reality bespeaks a less complicated time, before appropriation in the visual arts, digital sampling in music, Internet avatars, and reality TV was the norm. A photographic print was just that: an emulsified surface that clung to a piece of paper. Once out in the world, these physical artifacts tended to be stable objects like newspapers, photographic prints, and bound books. The only way to reconfigure them was with a razor blade and a pot of glue. But even then, they remained paper-bound stable artifacts. These copies often bore signs of their original context: a Xerox of a newspaper photograph, for instance, still carried benday dots and signature typefaces like Imperial in the *New York Times*. Photographs appearing on the pages of a newspaper had proper authorial accreditations and captions that made their sources readily identifiable and verifiable. Today, photographs emanating from newspaper websites are regularly reblogged without attribution or context; oftentimes the caption doesn't travel with the photograph, nor does authorial accreditation. These are free-floating artifacts, detached from the anchored signifiers and contexts that first birthed their meaning. A thousand new contexts and meanings emerge from the viral nature of photographic distribution in the digital age.

In "Jennifer in Paradise," Dullaart sees embodied a more

innocent and hopeful time: a time before the Internet was steeped in surveillance, when few worried about the politics behind software design, the digital divide, the colonizing of the digital commons, and the invasion of privacy; a time before social media and all the venom that came with it. It's a complicated image. While there's something touching and pure about it in an idealistic web 1.0 way, it's also filled with blind spots in terms of race, class, gender, and colonization.

In his artwork, Dullaart often warps Jennifer beyond recognition, radically applying Photoshop's own tools to her until the iconic image becomes an abstraction. His 2014 online video "Jennifer in Photoshop" is a loop of step-by-step Photoshop filters applied to the image until she is nothing more than a blur, then in reverse until she reappears in full resolution, set to the strains of Bobby Sherman's 1971 easy-listening song "Jennifer." In his artworks, Dullaart uses the image of Jennifer in Paradise without Knoll's permission, something that angered the developer when he found out about it. Knoll claimed, "I don't even understand what he's doing." But it seems like Knoll is the one who is lost, seemingly unable to grasp the full complexity of the forces his software package has unleashed, which is exactly the subject of Dullaart's work. When Jennifer was asked about Dullaart's art, she was sympathetic, offering a more realistic assessment: "The beauty of the Internet is that people can take things, and do what they want with them, to project what they want or feel."

A decade before Jennifer, a group of artists known as the

Pictures Generation critiqued the ways mass media images were reproduced and circulated. One of their primary tactics was to rephotograph preexisting photographs and claim them as their own. Inspired by the pop artists, who painted images of mass-produced consumer goods, the Pictures group wielded a camera instead of a paintbrush, entirely removing the hand of the artist. They called into question the nature of originality: can we say there is an original when it comes to an infinitely reproducible medium like photography? Their work was as much critique as it was practice. Long before the Internet, they questioned traditional ideas of authorship, setting the stage for today's image macros and memes. So you had Jeff Koons rephotographing billboards of brands like Hennessy and Nike and re-presenting them unaltered on the walls of galleries. Sherrie Levine rephotographed reproductions of Walker Evans's iconic black-and-white photos of Depression-era sharecroppers, then claimed she was the author of those images. Richard Prince did the same with Marlboro ads of leathery-skinned men on horseback in glorious natural settings of the American West. Simply by removing all ad copy and logos, and titling his series *Cowboys*, they were a sly reference to the dawn of the Reagan era, when the photos were made. All of these works asked the same question: if artists photograph an image— any image—aren't they the authors of that image? Certainly they pushed the button that created it. If blame is to be ascribed, perhaps the apparatus is guiltier than the artist.

Building on these earlier strategies, Richard Prince recently turned his eye to the Internet when he began appropriating other people's Instagram photos in a series entitled *New Portraits*. He downloaded them without permission, printed them out on large canvases, and hung them on gallery walls, adding only a few comments in the comment stream, which he printed along with the images. Each carried a price tag of $90,000. Upon hearing this, the Instagram community went nuts, accusing Prince of exploiting regular people's photographs for his own financial benefit. One Instagrammer whose work was reproduced by Prince said, "What Prince is doing is colonizing and profiting off a territory of the Internet that was created by a community of young girls," referring to the Instagram account of SuicideGirls, the alt-erotica stream with more than three million followers, from which Prince liberally poached. Yet what Prince did was perfectly legal. Instagram's privacy policy states: "Once you have shared User Content or made it public, that User Content may be re-shared by others." Those offended might have been wise to read Flusser. They were fooled into thinking that their Instagram feeds are private photo albums of their most beloved and cherished images, rather than a façade that feeds a series of voracious apparatuses. What was as remarkable as the amount of money he made from appropriating other people's photos was the fact that with this one small gesture, our naïveté about the apparatus was so sharply critiqued and exposed.*

---

* In December 2015, Prince was sued by the photographer Donald Graham for copyright infringement for reproducing a black-and-white image of a Rasta smoking a joint that Graham had posted on his Instagram, which Prince included in his *New Portraits* series.

In 2008, Prince made the series of paintings *Canal Zone*, which incorporated black-and-white photographs of Rastafarians that were taken by a little-known photographer named Patrick Cariou nearly a decade earlier. Prince took Cariou's photos and, like the Instagram pieces, blew them up large and printed them on canvas. But instead of just straight appropriations, he added and subtracted elements, at times cutting and pasting images on top of each other, other times isolating Cariou's images so that they floated in empty fields. Prince also painted heavily on top of some of the photos. In one of the most reproduced images from the series, Prince took a photo of a shirtless Rasta standing in a forest with dreadlocks draping down to the ground, and pasted George Harrison's Rickenbacker guitar in his hands. He also blotted out the Rasta's eyes and mouth with blue circles. The paintings generated more than $10 million worth of sales. Cariou, who made about $8,000, from his book, sued. The case went back and forth in court for several years, with the art world hoping for vindication of its long-standing tactics of appropriation, and the photography world hoping to regain control of their medium in a time of ubiquitous digital imagery. In 2013, the court decided in favor of Prince, saying he had transformed Cariou's photos and it was therefore considered fair use. The irony is that this battle was being played out during the digital age on two analog mediums: paintings stretched on canvas and photographs printed in books. At the heart of the case was neither painting nor money; it was photography, which Flusser presciently called "the mother of all reproducible apparatuses."

A few months ago, a friend pulled a book off of her bookshelf that was a new appropriation work by Prince, one as radical and daring as anything he'd done. The premise of the book was achingly simple: it was a reproduction of the first edition of *The Catcher in the Rye*, identical in every way to the iconic first edition, except that everywhere Salinger's name appeared, it was swapped for Prince's. The production value of the book was astonishingly high, a perfect facsimile of the original, right down to the thick, creamy paper stock; even the typeface on the book's pages was identical. The text on the dust jacket—replete with the familiar line drawing of the angry red horse—begins: "Anyone who has read Richard Prince's *New Yorker* stories, particularly *A Perfect Day for Bananafish, Uncle Wiggily in Connecticut, The Laughing Man*, and *For Esmé—with Love and Squalor*, will not be surprised by the fact that his first novel is full of children." It's a dead ringer through and through with the exception of the following disclaimer on the colophon page: "This is an artwork by Richard Prince. Any similarity to a book is coincidental and not intended by the artist." The colophon concludes with: ©Richard Prince.

For Prince, the book was modestly priced: a few hundred bucks for a limited unsigned edition, with a copy signed by Prince selling for several thousand, matching the identical price of what the signed first edition by Salinger goes for on that day. Remarkably, Prince took a bunch of copies of his pirated edition, spread them out on a blanket on the sidewalk in front of Central Park, and sold them for forty dollars each. It's unknown how many—if any—he sold or how a presumably befuddled public might have responded to this performance.

Prince is openly pirating what is rather valuable literary property—American literature—practically begging the estate of Salinger to sue him. One imagines that if Salinger's estate went after him, he'd have the money to settle with them. And, yet—probably because this is a low-profile, low-income-generating project—nothing ever happened. But this gesture, played out on a relatively small scale, on paper, is not really as much about Salinger as it is about the status of the cultural artifact in the digital age, its infinite reproducibility, and our changing notion of authorship and authenticity in the twenty-first century.

Images on the web take on a Wittgenstein-like character, flickering back and forth between the semantic and the visual, being both at once. We search for images based on key words that summon images, yet it's in this interval— between typing and clicking—that the correspondence between the two begins to slip. I enter the word "red" into Google Images and the first result is of a red square from

Wikipedia. I assume that the image is from the Wikipedia entry to the color "red" but when I go to the page, I find that it is, in fact, the entry for "Red flag (politics)," which reminds me of Wittgenstein's claim that "the two propositions, 'Red is a primary color' and 'Red is a color in many flags,' wear the same linguistic dress." The tension between language and image on the web is the subject of a recent project by the London-based artists King Zog (Felix Heyes and Benjamin West) called *Google, Volume 1,* which takes the entire *Oxford English Dictionary* and replaces every word with the first image displayed when searched on Google Images. The result is a 1,328-page tome that begins, obviously enough, with an image of an aardvark and ends with a mysterious scientific-looking diagram, which the book's index tells me is zymase, an enzyme that catalyzes sugars into ethanol and carbon dioxide.

When I search the book for the image "red" trying to find the *r*'s I flip through the pages and stumble across an image of a red flag—a Nazi flag, to be specific—and think that I have found the entry for "red." It is only when I look to one side of it and see an image of a "sweater," which is followed by a broom "sweeping" that I realize I'm looking at the entry for "swastika." I flip backward, then, trying to find the *r*'s and when I do, I land on the page with a poster for the movie *The Recruit*, followed by a medical illustration of a "rectum." Nearby, I see an image of an open book with the words "verso" and "recto" on it and I know I must be getting close. Sure enough, I turn the page and there is the image for "red," which is not a solid square of red referencing a red flag, as Google Images today tells me it is, but instead is a movie poster for a film called *Red*. Evidently back in 2013, the day the authors sought the first entry for "red" in Google Images, the movie poster was the top hit. Today, things have changed. Tomorrow—or even later this afternoon—the top hit on Google Images for "red" might very well change again. Printed in an edition of only three hundred copies, each subsequent edition will scoop the top images search terms from that printing date, resulting in an entirely different book each time it's published.

Baltimore-based artist Dina Kelberman produced a similar project called *I'm Google*, which is a collection of images she finds on the web and meticulously organizes according to their formal and lyrical properties. Displayed in a seemingly endless scroll, the project visually resembles both Google Images and Pinterest, which, according to her artist statement, "results visually in a colorful grid that slowly changes as the viewer scrolls through it. Images of houses being demolished transition into images of buildings on fire, to forest fires, to billowing smoke, to geysers, to bursting fire hydrants, to fire hoses, to spools of thread. The site is constantly updated week after week, batch by batch, sometimes in bursts, sometimes very slowly." At first glance, Kelberman's project feels like she created the most perfect algorithm, one that is able to match perfectly the semantic and visual qualities of images in the most poetic fashion. Yet the truth is that she's meticulously picking and arranging these images by hand, one after the next. In this way, she's closer to Christian Marclay's *The Clock* than she is Google's search function that allows you to find images that are visually similar images. Google is a smart formal algorithm but it misses the nuances of what only a human can bring to a project: humor, subtlety, irony, perversity, playfulness, and poetry. It's not enough to simply "raid the icebox," and display the treasures because they are there. Instead, it's Kelberman's artistic sensibility—her "order of the catalogue," as Walter Benjamin would put it—that makes a striking counterpoint to the "confusion of a library."

Over the course of the year when I was named MoMA's first poet laureate in 2013, I was fortunate enough to spend a lot of time in the museum among great works of art. Prior to my appointment, as a visitor, I would stand in front of certain paintings, lost for what seemed to be an eternity, completely oblivious of my surroundings. For me, the content of MoMA was its glorious collection; the apparatus surrounding the collection was something I barely noticed. But once I was there every week, I began to see how MoMA itself—its history and its narrative of modern art, the fact that it was MoMA—was influencing what I was looking at and the ways in which I was seeing it.

I found myself filtering my experiences through the lens

of "institutional critique," an art practice that like Flusser's apparatus takes as its subject matter the way institutions frame and control discourses surrounding the works of art they exhibit rather than focusing on the content of the works themselves. A more traditional approach would be to isolate a work of art and to appreciate its aesthetic values, while ignoring the context in which it is being displayed and the factors that brought it there. Like Flusser, institutional critique claims that the structures surrounding the works are actually what gives the work much of its meaning, oftentimes controlling the reception of a work in ways we as viewers are unaware of. While institutional critique began in the museum, the practice evolved over time to include everything from the production and distribution of art to an examination of the corporate offices or collectors' homes where the art was hung. By the 1980s, it roped in art criticism, academic lectures, and art's reception in the popular press. Around the same time, art schools began offering classes in poststudio practice, where the study of institutional critique became an act of making art in and of itself.

So you get works like Hans Haacke's 1970 *MoMA Poll*, which was literally a poll that asked viewers: "Would the fact that Governor Rockefeller has not denounced President Nixon's Indochina Policy be a reason for your not voting for him in November?" Haacke then provided two Plexiglas boxes into which the YES or NO ballots were cast. While, aesthetically, the piece fit into the information-based art of the period, Haacke meant to shed light on the fact that Nelson Rockefeller was a member of MoMA's board, thereby making visible the normally hidden play of money, power, and politics behind the institution. Another tactic is to take objects from a museum's collection and rearrange them in ways that highlight the biases of the collection. For instance, in 1993 the artist Fred Wilson critiqued the Maryland Historical Society's collection in relationship to Maryland's history of slavery. For this show, he regrouped specific objects from the museum in order to speak of, in Wilson's words, "a history which the museum and the community wouldn't talk about: the history of the exclusion and abuse that African-American people experienced in that area." Other works have focused on the physical institution itself. Andrea Fraser, a performance artist, often acts as a docent, leading groups at museums on false tours, not of the works on the walls, but of the security systems, water fountains, and cafeterias. In 2003, Fraser performed what was perhaps the ultimate work of institutional critique in which a collector paid twenty thousand dollars to sleep with her, "not for sex," according to Fraser, but "to make an artwork."

What I witnessed at MoMA was institutional critique, being performed not by artists, but by the museum's visitors. While I was there, I noticed something odd happening in front of *Les Demoiselles d'Avignon* and other paintings in the museum, something that signified radical shifts in the nature and structure of the museum itself brought on by technology. Instead of reverently standing there in front of Picasso's masterpiece, scads of visitors were turning their backs on the painting, snapping selfies, and uploading them to social media. I noticed that more visitors were paying attention to their devices than to the artwork on the walls. In every gallery, benches intended for the quiet contemplation of modernist masterpieces were co-opted by smartphone users hunched over their devices. While technology originally claimed to enhance the viewer's museum experience with one-way audio guides—those high-toned narrators walking you through the collection instructing you how to view the art—today technology works to destabilize the work on the walls. Instead of the official voice of the museum on people's headphones, now it's Beyoncé, NPR, Spotify, or any number of different podcasts.

This shift, driven by technology, is happening everywhere in culture now, from the massive open online courses (MOOCs) in higher education to crowdsourced knowledge bases like Wikipedia. In the museum, the artwork—along with the museum's once unassailable top-down museum narrative—for most visitors has become secondary to the experience of actually being there. The art on the walls is the pretense that draws people to the museum, but once they get there, they're elsewhere: on their smartphones, facebooking, instagramming, vineing, tweeting, periscoping, texting, facetiming—everything, really, except for paying full attention to the art on the walls. The artwork now often acts as a backdrop, evidence that proves to the world you were, in fact, there. Museums in general are alive and well—the Metropolitan Museum of Art reported a record 6.3 million visitors in 2014—but the function of the space has been transformed into a social rather than artistic one: a town square, a place to gather, a place to party, a place to dance, a place to hear music, a place to eat, a place to drink, a place to network, a place to be seen on First Wednesdays and Free Fridays.

CHAPTER 7

Lossy and Jaggy

Back in college in the late 1970s, I was never the kind of person who brought high-end audiophile equipment into the dorm. In those days, kids would show up to school with speakers the size of refrigerators, chunky solid-state receivers, and turntables that resembled chrome-plated turbine engines. They would set this stuff up to be blown away—literally—hoping to re-create the iconic 1978 Memorex ad in which a shaggy-haired dude in dark shades holds on to his chair for dear life as a hurricane of sound coming out of the speakers threatens to blow him straight back. Inevitably, these people had mediocre taste in music; they were more concerned with how their music sounded than with the music itself. Being a bit of a punk rocker, I tended to go in the opposite direction, listening to crummy lo-fi umpteenth-generation cassette tapes and scratched vinyl, which I played on a cheap all-in-one console that had a turntable, cassette player, radio, and two bottom-end speakers the size of Pop-Tarts boxes. It suited me just fine. I was raised on the trebly sound of AM radio squawking out of transistor radios: for me, if the music couldn't sound great coming out of tiny speakers, then it wasn't worth listening to. Later, when CDs came out, I plugged a Discman into that system and the CDs sounded no different than my LPs and cassettes, which sounded no different than the radio. All I heard was the music.

Little did I know that in the digital age, my listening habits would win out. In an era when music went portable, music went lo-fi. In order for it to soar across our networks and quickly settle on our devices, music had to lose a good chunk of its sound due to digital compression. While most of us can't really tell the difference between an MP3 and a CD—particularly when played over a portable device through tinny white earbuds—not everyone is thrilled about this. For years, Neil Young has grumbled about our digitally degraded audio experience, complaining that even our CDs are compromised. According to Young, they contain only 15 percent of the recording information found on the original analog master tracks. MP3s take that down to 5 percent. He even went so far as to make it the theme of a recent roaring half-hour jam called "Driftin' Back," which, like many Neil Young songs, is a paean to how much better things were in the past. "We live in the digital age," Young moans, "and unfortunately it's degrading our music, not improving."

What happened to the other 95 percent? It was knocked out by the compression it took to make MP3s tiny enough to fly across the networks. Uncompressed digital formats were full resolution: you got 100 percent of the sound but they were unwieldy and huge. In the 1990s scientists witnessing the explosive growth of the web began working on a solution that would create listenable audio files that would be small enough to be streamed or downloaded quickly. They used a technique they called lossy compression, in which redundant or unnecessary information was eliminated (hence the technological etymology: "loss"). When you rip a CD to MP3s, the encoder that converts your disc is a lossy one, removing all the sounds that are either humanly inaudible or are so close together the human ear can't discern one from another. The compression is a sleight of hand, resulting in a venetian blind version of the song: the missing pieces are then bridged by your ear and brain's natural ability to fill in the missing gaps, resulting in the illusion of full and continuous sound. In lossless compression formats like FLAC (Free Lossless Audio Codec)—good for downloading but not for streaming—the original, uncompressed data is re-created from the compressed version.

When MP3s were in development, the lossy technique was being tested on big, bombastic tracks like late 1950s Nelson Riddle–arranged Sinatra tunes. And they were sounding pretty good: there was so much going on in them that the missing information was unnoticeable. But one day, a scientist working on the compression algorithm was walking down a corridor in the lab and the radio was playing "Tom's Diner," Suzanne Vega's sparse 1981 a cappella song. He stopped and wondered how compression technology would sound on something this stripped down. He saw it as a litmus test for the technology: if an unadorned and unaccompanied human voice like Vega's was not noticeably altered when compressed, then anything else it was applied to would also pass. After some tinkering, it worked and as a result, the song earned Suzanne Vega the awkward title Mother of the MP3, presumably an appellation she never asked for.

Recently a doctoral music student named Ryan Maguire did a project called "The Ghost in the MP3" in which he took all of the audio that was removed from the MP3 compression on "Tom's Diner" and re-presented it as his own composition. Apropos of its title, it's an eerie thing. It's as if Vega's song was chopped into small pieces and then flung into outer space. You can still vaguely discern the structure of Vega's song but it's been disassembled and scattered, awash in faint echoes and lots of reverb. Shards of Vega's voice, interspersed with random digital glitches, come through loud and clear, then suddenly vanish without explanation. The overall feeling of Maguire's piece is indeed ghostly, like listening to the inverse of Vega's song or perhaps an avant-garde ambient remix of it.

Still, Neil Young is right: we're missing most of the richness from our listening experiences. But the surprise to that many people don't seem to mind. The marks technology leaves on our cultural artifacts—as ugly as they may be to some ears—become Proustian madeleines that plunge us down involuntary memory tunnels. From Phil Spector's 1960s Wall of Sound, to the chunky Fairlight synthesizers in eighties pop music, to the recent blur of Auto-Tune, entire generations get hooked on these musical tropes. Jonathan Berger, a music professor at Stanford, has noted that his students actually prefer the sound of MP3s to higher quality formats because they signified the sound—they call it the MP3s' "sizzle"—of their generation. This particular sound of MP3 compression is as much the hallmark of their youthful audio experience as the cracks and pops of vinyl were mine. When CDs came out, the sounds of LPs—skips and pops—were often dropped in as both nostalgic and ironic gestures, warming up the icy digital format. Sometimes, CDs began with the sound of a needle dropping onto a vinyl record, a reminder that new technologies are haunted by the ones that precede them.

The MP3 is the latest in a long line of compressed artifacts and technologies. For most people, the pleasures of portability—remember Apple's enticing tagline for the first-generation of iPods, "1,000 songs in your pocket"—have outweighed the full-spectrum listening experience we've lost. Meanwhile, Neil Young tried to remedy his 5 percent problem by developing his own audio format and player called Pono, which restored the full spectrum of missing audio in a semiportable way. It was met with mixed reviews at best: one focus group in a blindfold test couldn't tell the difference between the Pono and the iPhone, and when used with headphones, the sound of the MP3-based iPhone actually won out. Streaming music services aren't much better. In order to deliver their music swiftly, they have to compress it. Neil Young recently pulled his music from services like Spotify, claiming that "streaming has ended for me . . . It's about sound quality. I don't need my music to be devalued by the worst quality in the history of broadcasting or any other form of distribution . . . When the quality is back, I'll give it another look. Never say never." *

In the late nineteenth century, visual art set out to shatter romantic preindustrial notions of coherence. In an age when industrial products were being spit out piecemeal on an assembly line, how could one ever again depict the world as unified? So, in his still lifes, Cézanne painted all sides of an apple at once, putting an end to the idea that the world can be seen from our—and only our—point of view. Instead, all objects and ideas are open to multiple interpretations, a Pandora's box of possibilities. The ante was upped by the cubists who, taking Cézanne one step further, went from one individual seeing an object from many angles, to the many eyes of a crowd seeing many objects from many angles. Their shattered picture planes represented a fourth dimensional way of seeing, with all perspectives represented simultaneously. Theirs was a networked vision, harnessing the power

---

* Young's "never say never" may, in fact, be drawing to a close with streaming lossless FLAC files.

of the crowd as opposed to the isolation of the individual. In this way, cubism anticipated common computing ideas from crowdsourcing to "hive minds" and "swarm intelligences." They also were inspired by cinema, in both its experiments with rapid-fire montage and its mechanical mass distribution of imagery. In his book *The Language of New Media*, the historian Lev Manovich has eloquently written about how cinema is hardwired into the DNA of computing. Alan Turing's Universal Turing Machine, for instance, was operated by reading and writing numbers on an endless tape, similar to the way a projector reads data from celluloid film. It's no coincidence that one of the earliest computers, built in 1936 by the German engineer Konrad Zuse, was run off of discarded 35 mm movie film.

Similar to the cubists, the Italian futurists began incorporating primitive forms of animation in their paintings. Giacomo Balla's painting *Dynamism of a Dog on a Leash* (1912) shows a dachshund's feet blurred in a whir of motion. In fact, everything in the picture that is moving is depicted as such: the leash is like a series of ghostly threads waving multiple times through the air; the person's feet walking the dog consists of dozens of flying shoes; even the dachshund's tail is spinning out of control. Futurism celebrated motion-based technology, depicting frame by frame the speed of the motor car, the rhythmic pounding of the assembly line, and the *rat-a-tat* of the machine gun.

It's not a far cry from Balla's early twentieth-century oil on canvas depiction of motion to today's animated GIFs.

The GIF, like the lossy MP3, is a low-resolution format, known in computing terms as jaggy, named for the jagged-edged pixels you see when you zoom in on a lo-res image. Like flipbooks, animated GIFs are made by sequencing a series of still images, hearkening back to the earliest days of cinematic animation technologies like magic lanterns or zoetropes. The best animated GIFs are like pocket cinema, with narratives and punch lines, all unfurling in a matter of seconds, then infinitely looping. And because they have no sound, they have to express strong ideas entirely through visual images, the way silent films did in the early part of the twentieth century. Their brevity, too, has echoes of Edison and the Lumière Brothers, whose reels were often no longer than thirty seconds.

The animated GIF is haunted by earlier technologies like painting, cartoons, and cinema. Yet creating animated GIFs is a modern-day craft. Even today, there is no real shortcut to making a dazzling animated GIF, which still must be constructed more or less in a hands-on way. They're meticulously woven, frame by frame, much as they were two decades ago, which might help to explain why they're still cherished: the collaboration between human and machine has kept animated GIFs alive as a sort of technological folk art.

There's a theory that the moment something verges on obsolescence, it's also on the cusp of revival, ready to reincarnate itself into new forms and uses. For example, when the horse was rendered obsolete as a mode of transportation, it found a new role in recreation. Or, in a cellular age, when everyone carries a clock in their pocket, the wristwatch evolved from timekeeper to luxury status object.* And while magazines were once a source of information, today many have come to resemble highly produced coffee-table books, more to be browsed than read. In a similar way, just as the GIF was on the verge of being rendered obsolete by streaming video, it was taken up as an artisanal craft by a small community of GIF builders, who quietly refined them from a jaggy way of communicating information into an art form. Their jumpy lo-res frames had been transformed into lushly looping image streams, depicting a tremendous amount of rich information in an insanely compressed form. Whereas in the beginning they were used to convey actual messages, that task had been usurped by streaming video and Flash, so they were free to become playful and artistic, functioning very much the way that image macros do—visual devices for quick and punchy commentary.

It was at this point that they caught the attention of Tumblr founder David Karp, who was so dazzled by the new generation of animated GIFs, that he opened up his platform to them, spurring an explosion of them.Today, Tumblr claims to have twenty-three million animated GIFs uploaded to it each day, and Facebook, which recently started supporting the format, says that five million animations daily

---

* Although this might be changing with the introduction of the Apple Watch, which as of this writing has yet to catch on in a significant way.

are sent through its messaging app. Like emojis, they can convey a great deal of information in a compressed format, the proverbial picture worth a thousand words.

An animated GIF is what McLuhan termed cool media. All forms of low-resolution imagery are cool; all forms of high-resolution imagery are hot. Hollywood is hot; animated GIFs are cool. A hot medium does a lot of the work for you. In the cinema, you're presented with gigantic images in the highest resolution available. McLuhan claimed that as a result cinemagoers are passive spectators; with hi-res there's not much left to the sensual imagination. All the blanks are filled in for you; you just have to sit back and enjoy. Narrative complexities are carried particularly well in hot media. A sweeping story coupled with beautiful cinematography displayed on a gigantic screen is what we think of as an optimal film-going experience.

Low-resolution, or cool media, requires you to do some work, as in the case of MP3s, where your ear has to fill in the blanks in order to give you the illusion that you're hearing it in higher resolution. Visual forms of cool media include comic strips, in which your mind is forced to make the connections between sequential frames, or television in which your eye must patch the mosaic of benday dots in order to give the illusion of a coherent and rich visual experience. We could say that the entire Internet—a huge compression machine—is a cool medium, one that demands an endless amount of participation. In this way, cool media has a web-based DIY ethos, one that invites you to customize, tinker with, and remix its artifacts.

We could say that hot media is "strong" and that cool media is "weak." But in this case, strong doesn't mean good and weak doesn't mean bad; it's actually just the opposite. For the past decade, art historians Hito Steyerl and Boris Groys have written in favor of "weak images," claiming that in the digital age, a weak or cool artifact is more democratic than a strong or hot one. The Internet and the artifacts that circulate through it—MP3s, GIFs, JPEGs, AVIs—are all, relatively speaking, low-resolution or weak artifacts. What makes the weak artifact powerful is not its resolution or quality but its abundance and availability—the fact that everyone can possess it, whenever one pleases, often for little or no cost. Think of clicking on a freely available but weak lo-res YouTube video from the comfort of your home versus going out to a cinema to pay for a strong visual experience. Obviously they're completely different experiences, but Steyerl and Groys argue that the weak experience is stronger because of its low-impact economics and the sheer fact of its availability. Due to its high compression rates, even HD streaming video is weak as compared to broadcast HD or DVD video.

Of course this is nothing new: bootleg VHSs and street-stall DVDs have long been a part of the democratic nature of weak images, trading hands for a few dollars and shown under less-than-optimal conditions. Taking cues from both street culture and the counterculture, Steyerl frames the so-called weak image as a type of resistance against consumerism: "In the class society of images, cinema takes on the role of a flagship store. In flagship stores high-end products are marketed in an upscale environment. More affordable derivatives of the same images circulate as DVDs, on broadcast television, or online as poor images." Politically, she says, the strong image is on the side of "official" culture: capital and corporations. The "poor" image is on the side of "unofficial" culture: file sharing and individuals. Her classification of image quality takes a political turn: "The poor image is a rag or a rip; an AVI or a JPEG, a lumpen proletariat in the class society of appearances, ranked and valued according to its resolution. The poor image has been uploaded, downloaded, shared, reformatted, and reedited."

There's a humanistic strain to Steyerl's logic. File-sharing networks create communities, bridging people from all over the world through the exchange of cultural artifacts. And every time a film is ripped, reformatted, remixed, shared, subtitled, and resubtitled, that artifact bears a human trace, marked by human intention. In this way, these altered weak images are palimpsests, containing records of human experience in ways that official out-of-the-box culture, sealed and protected, can only bear one mark—that of the corporation.

Because weak artifacts are in circulation, they're useful and dynamic, as opposed to the moldering reels of 35 mm films that languish in the dark archives of institutions, trotted out on occasion as part of a film festival that few will see. The bootleg is distributed with use-value in mind. In the late 1960s, the Cuban director and screenwriter Julio García Espinosa wrote a manifesto called "For an Imperfect Cinema," in which he went so far as to claim that "perfect cinema—technically and artistically masterful—is almost always reactionary cinema." Perfect cinema was made by Hollywood; imperfect cinema could be made by anybody. "Film today," he complained, "no matter where, is made by a small minority for the masses." That would change with the advent of Super 8 cameras and escalate in the 1970s and '80s with the widespread availability of video recorders. But Espinosa was prophetic: in the YouTube age everybody— in the famous words of German conceptual artist Joseph Beuys—is an artist. Weak images, then, are popular images in that they can be made and viewed by the many. Because compression makes it possible for weak images to travel long distances efficiently, they lose information and gain speed. Steyerl claims that "this is precisely why they end up being perfectly integrated into an information capitalism thriving on compressed attention spans, on impression rather than immersion, on intensity rather than contemplation, on previews rather than screenings."

So the problem becomes one of quantity. Who has the time to consume all of these artifacts? It's all well and good that "everybody is an artist," but what use is it if no one will ever see your works? Boris Groys puts a twenty-first-century spin on Espinosa: "Whereas before, a chosen few produced images and texts for millions of readers and spectators, millions of producers now produce texts and images for a spectator who has little to no time to read or see them. Earlier . . . one was expected to compete for public attention. One was expected to invent an image or text that would be so strong, so surprising, and so shocking that it could capture the attention of the masses, even if only for a short span of time."

The GIF was succeeded by the JPEG, a compressed format that is able to render images with much greater finesse than its predecessor. The jaggy compression works similarly to the way lossy MP3s do, relying on human psychovisual systems to fill in missing information. When these images are printed, most of the information that makes them look good on the screen is lost, resulting in blocky pixelation, which is why our photographs don't look as good on paper as they do on our devices. But for some artists, the distortion of low resolution (a cool or weak image) is a gateway to twenty-first-century abstraction.

Since 2007, the German photographer Thomas Ruff has taken jaggy low-resolution JPEGs from the web and blown them up to monumental proportions, exhibiting them as framed megaphotographs. His process is one of devaluation: he takes JPEGs from the web and renders them even lower resolution than he found them, compressing them further so that they are, in his words: "worst possible quality JPEGS. Then I get my image." The dramatic change in scale—from a thumbnail to more than seven feet tall—is shocking, as is his subject matter, which runs the gamut from porn to images of disaster from news sites, such as the burning Twin

Towers or Baghdad during the shock and awe siege. Like Steyerl's weak AVIs or Professor Berger's students who love the sizzle of MP3s, Ruff's photographs are a play of human intervention and technology's fingerprint. When blown up so large, you can really see the compression algorithm at work, as any semblance of visual cohesion is overwhelmed by the complex shades of pixelation at play. One thing these photos reveal is that the underlying structure of our digital images is the grid, a rather basic system of binaries, which when run through an algorithm trick the eye into patching together a seamless image. Because of the play between an iconic image like 9/11 and the blocky pixelation, Ruff's photographs flicker back and forth between realism and abstraction, being both and yet neither.

For his *Nudes* (1999), giant blowups of porn JPEGs dissolve objects of desire into pixelated nightmares. Ruff seems to be saying that on the web, porn—up close and enlarged—is nothing more than a pile of pixels, an illusion. What fuels your fantasies is technology, not flesh. When you see works from *Nudes* from across the room you see a coherent image of eroticism, but the closer you get, the more they fall apart. By the time you're standing in front of them you feel like Austin Powers when he realizes that the beautiful women surrounding him are not women at all, but are actually fembots.

Ruff's work reifies compression technology as the basis for an artistic investigation, one that is at the heart of our daily experience. He asks, "How much visual information is needed for image recognition? A pretty small quantity of data will go a long way for the brain and the computer, both of which take shortcuts for the sake of speedy comprehension . . . Our brain is very brilliant; at interpreting even the lowest resolution, it creates images."

CHAPTER 8

The Writer as Meme Machine

"It was while looking at Google's scan of the Dewey Decimal Classification system that I saw my first one—the hand of the scanner operator completely obscuring the book's table of contents," writes the artist Benjamin Shaykin. What he saw disturbed him: it was a brown hand resting on a page of a beautiful old book, its index finger wrapped in a hot-pink condom-like covering. In the page's lower corner, a watermark bore the words "Digitized by Google."

Shaykin was an MFA student in graphic design at the Rhode Island School of Design when he was given an assignment to choose a book from Brown University's library that would serve as the basis for a series of projects. Even though he had the physical books readily available, he found it easier, as many people do, to access them through Google Books. Once he came across the first hand, he was hooked, and started digging deeper into Brown's Special Collections library, which was digitized by Google. He came upon many more anomalies. "In addition to hands and fingers, I found pages scanned through tissue paper, pages scanned while midturn, and foldout maps and diagrams scanned while folded," he explained. "The examples were everywhere. I quickly became obsessed, and filled my hard drive with gigabytes of downloaded PDFs." He collected his strangest findings in a book called *Google Hands*, which ended up as one in a series of a dozen small hand-sewn books, each focused on a different type of glitch. Through social media, he came into contact with like-minded collectors, and they began swapping artifacts.

There are several collections of Google hands around the web, each one as creepy as the one Shaykin saw. A small but thriving subculture is documenting Google Books' scanning process in the form of Tumblrs, printed books, photographs, online videos, and gallery-based installations. Something new is happening here that brings together widespread nostalgia for paperbound books with our concerns about mass digitization. Scavengers obsessively comb through page after page of Google Books, hoping to stumble on some glitch that hasn't yet been unearthed. This phenomenon is most thoroughly documented on a Tumblr called "The Art of Google Books," which collects two types of images: analog stains that are emblems of a paper book's history and digital glitches that result from the scanning. On the site, the analog images show scads of marginalia written in antique script, library DATE DUE stamps from the midcentury, tobacco stains, wormholes, dust motes, and ghosts of flowers pressed between pages. On the digital side are pages photographed while being turned, resulting in radical warping and distortion; the solarizing of woodcuts owing to low-resolution imaging; sonnets transformed by software bugs into pixelated psychedelic patterns; and the ubiquitous images of workers' hands.

The obsession with digital errors in Google Books arises from the sense that these mistakes are permanent, on the record. In 2013, Judge Denny Chin ruled that Google's scanning, en masse, of millions of books to make them searchable is legal. In the future, more and more people will consult Google's scans. Because of the speed and volume with which Google is executing the project, the company can't possibly identify and correct all of the disturbances in what is supposed to be a seamless interface. There's little doubt that generations to come will be stuck with both these antique stains and workers' hands.

Paul Soulellis is the proprietor of the Library of the Printed Web, which is housed in a pristine industrial space in Long Island City. Soulellis, a graphic designer turned book artist, has built a library that consists entirely of stuff pulled off the web and bound into paper books. One book is nothing more than dozens of images of highways rendered flat by flaws in Google Earth's mapping algorithm. There are grubby, stapled zines consisting of printed Twitter feeds, books of CAPTCHAs (an acronym for "Completely Automated Public Turing test to tell Computers and Humans Apart") presented as visual poetry, collections of photos of dogs with glowing eyes culled from Flickr, and lots of books where "photographers" have selected uncanny moments from Google Street View. While most of them are cheap, print-on-demand editions, a few are highly produced art books. One of the most beautiful books in the library is a collection of hundreds of crummy JPEGs of variations on the *Mona Lisa* (think the *Mona Lisa* morphed with E.T., made by a fourteen-year-old), printed on thick, handmade paper, and accordion folded into an expensive slipcase; the combination of the crappy and the crafted is weirdly effective. Then there are absurdly large projects, such as a ninety-six-volume set called *Other People's Photographs*, which scoops up material from random Flickr pages.

Amusing and titillating as these images are, it's easy to forget that they're the work of an army of invisible laborers—the Google hands. This is the subject of an art work by the Brooklyn-based artist Andrew Norman Wilson called *Scan-Ops*. The project began in 2007, when Wilson was contracted by a video-production company to work on the Google campus. He noted sharp divisions between the workers; one group, known as ScanOps, were sequestered in their own building. These were data-entry workers, the people to whom those mysterious hands belonged. Wilson became intrigued by them, and began filming them walking to and from their ten-hour shifts in silence. He was able to capture a few minutes of footage before Google security busted him. In a letter to his boss explaining his motives, Wilson remarked that most of the ScanOps workers were people of color. He wrote, "I'm interested in issues of class, race and labor, and so out of general curiosity, I wanted to ask these workers about their jobs." In short order, he was fired.

His video later became an art installation called *Workers Leaving the Googleplex*, a play on the title of the first film ever shown in public, the Lumière brothers' *Workers Leaving the Lumière Factory* (1895), as well as a remake by the German filmmaker Harun Farocki simply called *Workers Leaving the Factory* (1995). Wilson's Google experiences have also resulted in a series of beautiful gallery installations, with large, saturated color photos of those same workers' hands. Wilson reminds us that we, too, are contributing our own labor to the company's bottom line. He writes, "Everyone who uses the free Google perks—Gmail, cloud-storage, Google Books, Blogger, YouTube—becomes a knowledge worker for the company. We're performing freestyle data entry. Where knowledge is perceived as a public good, Google gathers its income from the exchange of information and knowledge, creating additional value in this process. Google, as we know it and use it, is a factory."

Soulellis calls the Library of the Printed Web "an accumulation of accumulations," much of it printed on demand. In fact, he says that "I could sell the Library of the Printed Web and then order it again and have it delivered to me in a matter of days." Since the advent of electronic readers, there's been a lot of hand-wringing about the demise of the printed page. And for a while, it looked like things were headed in one direction as bookstores folded and e-book sales soared. In an unanticipated twist, in 2015 e-book sales began slowing and print sales began climbing again. It turns out that people read both formats—the Kindle on the train and the paper version at home. In addition, cheap print-on-demand services like Lulu, which offer free PDFs along with physical copies for sale of any given title, have made it possible for people to publish and to buy the kinds of books Soulellis traffics in and proves once again that we're neither one way nor the other. Straddling the physical and the digital, we're inhabiting many spaces at the same time in ways that were unthinkable just a decade ago.

What if the poetic has left the poem in the same way Elvis has left the building? Long after the limo pulled away, the audience was still in the arena screaming for more, but poetry escaped out the back door and onto the Internet, where it is taking on new forms that look nothing like poetry. Poetry as we know it—sonnets or free verse on a printed page—feels akin to throwing pottery or weaving quilts, activities that continue in spite of their cultural marginality. But the Internet, with its swift proliferation of memes, is producing more extreme forms of modernism than modernism ever dreamed of.

These are the ideas of the Canadian media scholar Darren Wershler, who has been making some unexpected connections between meme culture and contemporary poetry. "These artifacts," Wershler claims, "aren't conceived of as poems; they aren't produced by people who identify as poets; they circulate promiscuously, sometimes under anonymous conditions; and they aren't encountered by interpretive communities that identify them as literary." Examples include a Nigerian e-mail scammer who writes out the entire *Harry Potter and the Chamber of Secrets* in longhand, a data engineer who renders the entire text of *Moby Dick* into emoticons, and a library scientist who converts *Ulysses* into QR codes.

Wershler calls these activities "conceptualism in the wild," referring to the aspect of 1960s conceptual art that concerned reframing, and thereby redefining, the idea of artistic genius (think of Duchamp's urinal). Conceptual projects of the period were generated by a kind of pre-Internet OCD, such as Sol LeWitt's exhaustive photographic documentation of every object, nook, and cranny in his Manhattan loft, or Tehching Hsieh's yearlong practice of taking a photo of himself every hour, on the hour. Today's conceptualists in the wild make those guys look tame. It's not uncommon to see blogs that recount someone's every sneeze since 2007, or of a man who shoots exactly one second of video every day and strings the clips together in time-lapse mashups. There is a guy who secretly taped all his conversations for three years and a woman who documents every morsel of food she puts into her mouth. While some of these people aren't consciously framing their activities as works of art, Wershler argues that what they're doing is so close to the practices of sixties conceptualism that the connection between the two can't be ignored.

And he's right. Younger writers find it stimulating: they

are reclaiming this "found" poetry and uploading it to the self-publishing platform Lulu. They create print-on-demand books that most likely will never be printed but will live as PDFs on Lulu—their de facto publisher and distributor. These are big, ridiculous books, like a 528-page book that reprints every single tweet that contains the word "McNugget"; or a book that appropriates more than 400 pages' worth of Discogs listings of small-bit session players from long-forgotten 1970s LPs; or a project that converts Gertrude Stein's difficult modernist text *Tender Buttons* into illegible computer code; or a fifty-eight-page list poem of poets' names followed by their presumed economic status: "John Ashbery is a rich poet." "Amiri Baraka is comfortable."

Quality is beside the point. This type of content is about the quantity of language that surrounds us, and about how difficult it is to render meaning from such excesses. In the past decade, writers have been culling the Internet for material and making books that are more focused on collecting than on reading. It's not clear who, if anyone, actually reads these, although they are often cited by other writers working in the same mode. There are few critical systems in place to identify which books are better than others. For now, these authors function on a flat, horizontal field creating a communitarian body of work in which one idea or one author is interchangeable with another.

This ethos is evident on the smart art blog the Jogging, where artworks in the form of JPEGs are posted semi-anonymously and, like all blogs, last only until they are pushed off the page by newer works. It is an ephemeral amnesiac data flow, one that swaps the art world's market-driven frenzy for networked global visibility. On the Jogging, it isn't really the individual posts that count: the blog's métier lies in its ceaseless and restless stream of information.

The best images on the Jogging are the ones that walk a fine line between sharp humor and weird ambiguity, such as a hacked black-and-white iconic photo of Fidel Castro chomping on his famous cigar. The only alteration the artist made to the found image is a photoshopped blue dot at the end of his cigar. The title is the reveal: *Che Guevara Smoking an E-Cig*. Not obviously funny enough to be a meme, it's a sly twenty-first-century mutation of a twentieth-century icon, one that welds critiques of power, commodity, history, advertising, and technology into an Internet readymade. Another image is entitled *wlan router under water*, which shows exactly that: two wireless routers photoshopped onto the floor of a swimming pool while the legs of swimmers dangle nearby. It looks like something out of *Jaws*, ciphered through the digital age. The surreal warping of entertainment and technology—hallmarks of the Jogging—conflate leisure with danger: Wouldn't plugged-in routers electrocute everyone in the water, killing them faster than sharks would? Or is this a new technology that allows Wi-Fi underwater so that the swimmers could tweet while diving? For now, it's a sci-fi idea, but in the forthcoming "Internet of things"—where intelligent everyday objects such as appliances communicate with one another over the web—we'll surely be able to tweet underwater while swimming via a network that's hardwired into the architecture of a pool.

These works are meant to be quickly favorited, re-blogged, and forgotten. They embrace the blips and flickers of the screen, celebrating the life span of a meme as a metric for artistic legacy. Yet the irony is that because the blog ended in 2014, they are now preserved for eternity—or at least until somebody pulls the plug on Tumblr. By then the images hosted there will have been indexed, spidered, and mirrored so many times that their eradication will be virtually impossible, ensuring them a place in a virtual pantheon. In the twentieth century, many artists who claimed to want to burn down museums ended up enshrined in them. The same remains true for the twenty-first: young artists wishing to skirt conventional valorization by the art establishment have, by posting their works on the web, inadvertently become preserved for posterity by the search engine.

Fifty years ago, when Andy Warhol said things like "I want to be a machine" and "It's easier not to care," he was romanticizing the formal and emotional cleanliness of machine-based production. Humans, after all, court messiness. Warhol's salvo is extended by today's Internet poets, who resemble zombies more than inspired bards, gathering and shoveling hoards of inert linguistic matter into programs, flipping switches, letting it rip, and producing poetry on the scale of WikiLeaks cables. Imagine the writer as a meme machine, writing works with the intention for them to ripple rapidly across networks only to evaporate as quickly as they appear. Imagine poetry that is vast, instantaneous, horizontal, globally distributed, paper thin, and, ultimately, disposable.

R. Sikoryak is a graphic novelist who has been drawing unoriginal comics for more than a quarter of a century. Inspired by a mix of *Raw* magazine (to which he contributed) and John Cage (he once drew a strip version of Cage's aleatory work *Indeterminacy*), Sikoryak meticulously redraws well-known historical comics and mashes them up with classic works of literature. His book *Masterpiece Comics* includes strange works like Dante's *Inferno* drawn as a series of Bazooka Joe bubblegum comics, and Camus's *The Stranger* as the story line for a *Superman* strip.

His most recent project takes a more conceptual twist. This time, instead of classic literature, he's matched appropriated comics with the complete text of the iTunes Terms and Conditions for a total of seventy pages, published in three comic books. "Instead of taking an important book that no one has read," Sikoryak says, "I've taken an agreement that none of us have read and have made an unreadable book out of it." All of the classic comics protagonists—Charlie Brown, Dilbert, Spider-Man, Richie Rich—have been redrawn to resemble Steve Jobs, replete with scraggly beard and round glasses. Each page presents a different cartoon style; every source is cited in a bibliography in the back of the book. There are lovely details: Snoopy's doghouse is branded with an Apple logo; Hellboy, posing as Jobs, is battling a monster listening to an iPod with white earbud cords dangling from his head.

Why would someone want to do this? Sikoryak, when I asked him, had an avant-garde response: "What would be the most absurd text to put into a comic, the least likely thing to do?" He also selected the legal code because—somewhat surprisingly, given the nature of his work—he's never had any legal problems. This got him wondering whether those miles of tiny legal print ever really amount to anything.

Sikoryak's book also speaks to how, after decades of scanning, file sharing, and cutting and pasting, notions of copyright and authorship in the comics world have relaxed. Bill Kartalopoulos, a comics historian and series editor of the *Best American Comics* series, told me that pirating, copying, bootlegging, and plagiarism have been around since the beginning of modern comics history. "The foundational nineteenth-century graphic novels of Swiss cartoonist Rodolphe Töpffer were pirated in France, England, and elsewhere," Kartalopoulos says. "At that time, if the French wanted to produce a pirated edition of Töpffer's Swiss book, someone would literally have to redraw and re-engrave his images onto wood blocks. Later, in the nineteen-thirties and forties, small bootleg comic books called 'Tijuana Bibles'— also referred to at the time as 'Fuck Books'—were sold under the table, featuring famous cartoon characters like Popeye and Little Orphan Annie in explicit sexual situations that didn't normally present themselves on the daily newspaper page."

By the sixties and seventies, with the counterculture in full swing, everyone from the situationists—who whited out speech balloons and filled them with political text—to the Air Pirates, a collective of Bay Area hippies, were copying and repurposing famous comic strips. The Air Pirates adopted the styles of an array of historical cartoonists as their own (including *Krazy Kat* artist George Herriman and turn-of-the-century cartoonist Frederick Burr Opper). In *Air Pirates Funnies*, they took on the Disney entertainment empire and redrew Mickey, Minnie, and company Tijuana Bible–style: smuggling drugs and having orgies. Wanting to stick it to the man, they made sure Disney was aware of their activities. Disney, predictably, sued. They later settled with Air Pirate Dan O'Neill and made him promise never to draw Mickey Mouse again.

Thirty-year-old Blaise Larmee may best exemplify that stick-it-to-the-man attitude. Mostly, he uses web platforms to mess with the comics establishment. Modeling his practice on the situationists, he adores misattribution, altering other people's comics by inserting his own texts into speech balloons, which end up getting reblogged as authentic artifacts. He once pretended he was named editor for *Best American Comics* and posted his announcement on a bogus Chris Ware Tumblr he created. He added a note that promised: "If you reblog this Tumblr image, your work will be included in the book." Asked why he does these things, he answers, "Because I can."

His most perplexing work may be *Labor Day Comic*, a series of screenshots of mundane tasks that he performed on his computer over the course of one Labor Day. He strung these images, one after another, onto a blog, and called it a comic strip. Frame by frame, we watch him download a Vangelis album from MediaFire—taking screen caps every step of the way—then uploading these images to Flickr, and finally posting the whole process to Blogger. The title suggests a political edge: is this what labor looks like now?

The Greek artist Ilan Manouach takes a more directly political stance in his work. He's most famous for his book *Katz*, which is a reinterpretation of Art Spiegelman's *Maus* except that all the characters—Nazis, Jews, Poles—are drawn with cats' heads. (In the original, Jews are drawn as mice, while non-Jewish Germans and Poles are drawn as cats and pigs, respectively.) Besides this, not a single word or image was added or removed. The book caught the legal ire of Spiegelman's French publisher, Flammarion, and the entire run of one thousand copies was pulped. He did something similar with *Les Schtroumpfs noirs* (*The Black Smurfs*), a comic originally published in 1963. In the story, a Smurf village is infected by a black fly that bites all the villagers, turning them from their natural blue color to black, and making them go mad. A cure is finally found and every Smurf is restored to blue. When the book was later turned into an animation, the Smurfs were changed from black to purple to avoid the racial subtexts. Manouach made a facsimile of the original, but transposed each of the book's four colors onto the cyan plate, resulting in a book that is entirely blue.

For his most recent project, *Tintin Akei Kongo*, Manouach took the most popular Tintin adventure in Francophone Africa, *Tintin au Congo* (1931), and had it translated for the first time into Lingala, the official Congolese dialect, without the permission of the publisher. The pirated book will never officially be distributed in the Democratic Republic of the Congo—only one hundred copies have been brought to Kinshasa so far—but for Manouach: "It's the idea, the provocation, the critique, that is important." Manouach sees himself as an agitator, a sort of Hans Haacke of the comics world. Trained as a conventional comic book artist, he grew restless by what he perceived to be the limits of the comics world. "There's not much critical discourse in comics and not much questioning of convention," he says. "Instead, there's a lot of nostalgia, which has kept comics politically and aesthetically conservative."

"Certainly there are many issues connected to fair use that are still in flux, and these artists are all troubling those waters in interesting ways," says Kartalopoulos. "Comics have historically been considered part of commercial popular culture, and existed to the side of modernist developments for much of the twentieth century. What's most exciting to me is that now there is a growing critical mass of well-rounded comics artists who are comfortably bringing their avant-garde legacy to the form." There is also, these days, a renewed sense of the political power of cartooning, in the wake of the attack on *Charlie Hebdo* and the debates that have followed. These artists' strategies—Sikoryak's remixings, Manouach's recontextualizations, Larmee's provocations— bring a contemporary set of conceptual tools to the making of comics, tools that could prove helpful in navigating the swift-moving waters of the Internet age.

The Internet is indeed changing our ways of reading and writing. Few want to read *War and Peace* sitting in front of a computer screen; it's the wrong place for in-depth, lengthy reading, which is better done offline, either on paper or on our devices. When we are in front of a computer hitched to a fast web connection, the last thing we want to do is stop, slow down, and do only one thing. Idling on a highway is antithetical to the medium. Instead, our time in front of a machine is active time: we're clicking and seeking, harvesting and communicating. Our ways of reading and writing, then, while on the web, reflect this active state. Offering coping strategies, any number of articles tell us to keep our e-mails short, that lengthy e-mails will most likely go unread. They offer suggestions like "commit to making every message five sentences long—or less" and "treat all email responses like SMS text messages, using a set number of letters per response." The migration to short forms of writing and reading that we're witnessing—shorter e-mails, tweets,

SMS messages—are the latest in a long line of compressed language: hieroglyphs, ideograms, haiku, Morse code, telegrams, newspaper headlines, the old Times Square news zipper, advertising slogans, concrete poems, and desktop icons.

Writing on electronic platforms is transforming aspects of our daily communication into constraint-based writing, a method of writing according to preordained rules initially explored in the 1960s and '70s by a group of French writers who called themselves the Oulipo (*Ouvroir de littérature potentielle* / Workshop of Potential Literature). They devised formulas for writing that were more akin to mathematics than they were to literature. A famous Oulipian constraint is called n+7, which involves replacing each noun in a text with the seventh one following it in a dictionary, so that the Declaration of Independence run through an n+7 operation, as the poet Rosmarie Waldrop did in her poem "Shorter American Memory of the Declaration of Independence" begins: "We holler these trysts to be self-exiled that all manatees are credited equi-distant, that they are endured by their Creditor with cervical unanswerable rims." The writer, bound by the constraints, accepts the results, regardless of how unappealing they may be to one's own literary sensibilities. Perhaps the most well known work of Oulipo writing is Georges Perec's *La disparition,* a 300-page novel that never uses the letter *e.* (The English translation of the book, *A Void,* which also doesn't contain the letter *e,* is an equally stunning feat.) Other methods used by the group include anagrams, palindromes, and Fibonacci sequences.

By swapping more traditional compositional methods

for mechanically inspired ones, the Oulipo anticipated some of the ways we'd use language in the digital age. Every time we tweet, using a 140-character constraint, we could be said to be composing an Oulipian poem. When Twitter gives us a constraint, we agree to comply with it, bending our language to suit its agenda. Few people throw up their arms and say, "I'm refusing to write in 140 characters. I will only write in 190 characters." Instead, by adapting ourselves to its platform, we find it a perfectly adequate way to express ourselves under a tight constraint. The parameters of Twitter are far from arbitrary: the 140-character constraint emerged from SMS culture, in which the standard character limit is 160 characters, minus 20 characters for the username.

People often grumble that on the web we've lost the craftsmanship of writing. But on Twitter, I often see a great deal of craft going into the composition of tweets. The constraint alone brings craft to the fore: how can I say something with such limited real estate? And then there is the game of the compositional method itself: watching the character count dwindle, then precisely editing and revising the tweet so it will fit into its allotted space. We substitute ampersands for "ands," delete commas, double spaces, and redundant words, use hashtags, and employ URL shorteners to craft the most compressed language possible. Many of our tweets go through this highly edited process, finally arriving at a perfect tweet, one in which a punchy statement is made with no characters left. Sometimes at the end of this process when we hit Send, we feel like we've posted a small literary jewel.

Twitter doesn't come with a how-to manual. We learn it by playing it. We tailor our writing to the game: be pithy, be clever, be polemical, and there's a chance you'll be read and retweeted; be mundane, be dull, only retweet others, and you'll most likely be on the lower end of the game. As novelist Sheila Heti put it, "You know within a matter of seconds if your tweet was successful." Twitter is reminiscent of Wittgenstein's concept of language games, in which he tried to tease out the unwritten rules of how we use language. Wittgenstein conceived of language as a board game involving, at the minimum, two players: a sender and a receiver. Speaking a sentence, he said, is like moving a piece on a board; the other player's response is the next move. What ensues is a conversation, an elaborate demonstration of the rules, structures—and inevitably, the faults and failings—of human language. Almost like an alien discovering language for the first time—William S. Burroughs referred to language as "a virus from outer space"—Wittgenstein questioned basic linguistic tenets: how our rules were developed, acquired, accepted, their various uses, and importantly, how they can be broken. A language game, Wittgenstein informs us, is a delicate one: failure to play well will result in potentially tragic misunderstanding.

Social media sets up the game board, gives you the structure, pieces, and a stage on which to play, but outside of some underlying rules—edicts prohibiting impersonation, violence, threats, violation of copyright, etc.—it comes with no instructions. Like language itself, its norms evolve through community engagement; trial and error shows what works (what people respond to well) and what doesn't. The rules of the game continually change with the platform, which is constantly tweaked to accommodate those ever-evolving rules, along with user feedback and investor concerns. The language itself inscribed into the interface is determinative of the platform's tenor. The word "follower" on Twitter or Instagram means something very different than Facebook's "friend." Followers imply that there are leaders—a vertically quantifiable power dynamic—whereas the concept of friendship is more ambiguous and horizontal. On Twitter and Instagram, there's always someone with more followers than you, making them more powerful than you, as opposed to Facebook's limit of five thousand friends, an accomplishment attainable by many, therefore roughly democratic at heart.* While we often use Twitter followers as a metric of power, we rarely do the same with Facebook friends. Followers, a synonym for sycophants, are endlessly expansive, emphasizing the underlying cutthroat power dynamic in play.

These same power dynamics are expressed throughout some of the most popular forums in digital culture. Take the tech blog Boing Boing, for instance. They're one of the most visible blogs on the web, but they create very little original content. Rather they act as a filter for the morass of information, pulling up the best stuff. The fact of Boing Boing

---

* It seems inevitable that Facebook will increase its five thousand friends limit.

linking to something far outweighs the thing they're linking to. The culture of citation and name-checking on the web has resulted in a cascade of "*re-*" gestures: *re*tweeting, *re*blogging, *re*gramming, and *re*posting. Good citation determines the worth of, say, your blog or your Twitter feed, warping the once-disdained idea of name-dropping into a widespread, powerful practice.

Social media is an economy of citation rather than engagement. For instance, on a larger Twitter feed—which is connected to the site of avant-garde artifacts I've run for the past two decades—we'll tweet out something very obscure, lengthy, or difficult. Within a matter of moments, it's been retweeted dozens of times. No one had the time to actually engage with what we've tweeted, rather it's something they've heard or knew about—name-checking—and were eager to pass along to their followers. Twitter's tweet activity dashboard shows this to be true. On a tweet that had 31,861 impressions, was retweeted 151 times, and liked 245 times, there was only 66 actual engagements with the content I was linking to. And from that one tweet, the feed only garnered one new follower. This point is made in an even more direct way when I mistweet a broken link. No matter. Broken link and all, it's still retweeted ad infinitum.

While word of mouth has always been the way certain types of information have been passed along, in the digital world, strong cultural capital is accumulated being the originator of something that is widely retweeted or regrammed. As social media evolves, it gets twitchier, chart-

ing micromovements in ever-subtler ways—I now see who
has retweeted a tweet I have retweeted—which keeps us in
the game tallying up the likes and glued to the screen.

Twitter's linguistic roots lie deep in modernism. James
Joyce's *Finnegans Wake*, perhaps the most unreadable book
ever written has, uncannily, set the stage for hashtags. Joyce's
book, published in 1939, was written as a linguistic dream-
scape (it was labeled by one critic as "dreamspeak"), one
that sought to bring the language of dreams and sleep to
the page. To write the *Wake*, Joyce crammed notebooks with
random thoughts and snippets of language he heard spoken
on the street, on the radio, or read in newspapers, which
became so dense and thick that even Joyce himself, with his
notoriously bad eyesight, couldn't decipher them. Instead, he
began transcribing exactly what he saw in its messy state to
a typewritten page. He then further mangled the language
by splitting up some words and recombining others, forming
complex compound words, not dissimilar to the way the German language works. So you get compound neologisms like
supershillelagh, happygogusty, soundhearing, smellsniffing,
and neverheedthemhorseluggarsandlistletomine. They're all
readable; you just have to be patient and read them closely, carefully deciphering each word. Because hashtags and
URLs allow no spaces, compound words became necessary.
Some examples of long, Joycean domains are:

*http://www.thelongestdomainnameintheworldand
thensomeandthensomemoreandmore.com/*

*http://www.abcdefghijklmnopqrstuvwxyzabcdefghi
jklmnopqrstuvwxyzabcdefghijk.com/*

*http://llanfairpwllgwyngyllgogerychwyrndrobwlll
lantysiliogogogoch.co.uk/* (named after a Welsh village)

*http://3.14159265358979323846264338327950
28841971693993751058209749 44592.com/* (the first
sixty-five numbers of pi)

Throughout *Finnegans Wake*, Joyce punctuated the text
with ten one-hundred-letter words that he called thunder-
claps, which are comprised of words in various languages
etymologically, visually, and aurally that relate to the theme
of thunder. He uses these words to break up the book into
several chapters, referring to various periods of cultural history, from the fall of Adam and Eve:

*bababadalgharaghtakamminarronnkonnbronntonnerron
ntuonnthunntrovarrhounawnskawntoohoohoordenen
thurnuk*

. . . to Thor, the Norse god of thunder . . .

*Ullhodturdenweirmudgaardgringnirurdrmolnirfenrirluk
kilokkibaugimandodrrerinsurtkrinmgernrackinarockar*

. . . which has 101 letters, and is thus able to fit in a
140-character tweet with thirty-nine characters left to spare.
The first Twitter hashtag, published by the former Goo-

gle designer Chris Messina in 2007, was #barcamp, referring to a technology conference called BarCamp. Notice, though, how Messina dropped the capital letters, making it less readable and more perplexing; by stripping out the capitals, he landed himself squarely in Joycean territory. Today, Twitter and Instagram are flooded with words that could be straight out of the *Wake*: #photooftheday, #follow4follow, #iphoneonly, #dylanobrienfanpage, or #themazerunnermovie.

Aping the speed of technology, linguistic compression was at the heart of modernism. In 1906, the anarchist art critic Félix Fénéon published anonymously composed three-line novellas as filler in the Paris daily newspaper *Le Matin*. They were intended as sidebars or distractions to the bigger stories of the day, compressed as digestible sound bites of the day's news:

> *Responding to a call at night, M. Sirvent, café owner of Caissargues, Gard, opened his window; a rifle shot destroyed his face.*

> *On the stake where they tied him up, four amateur policemen beat with sticks the young thief Dutoit, of Malakoff, whom they caught.*

> *As her train was slowing down, Mme. Parlucy, of Nanterre opened up and leaned out. A passing express cracked both her skull and the door.*

Fénéon's *faits divers* were much more than newspaper filler. Delicately meshing form with function, they were tiny poems in the guise of compressed Zolaesque potboilers, meant to quietly explode on the newspaper page where they were snuggled among more "important" stories. Intended to fly under the radar, they were subversive and, like well-honed tweets, gorgeously crafted. It's no wonder that a century later they'd be recognized as poetry. Predictably, Fénéon's "novellas" today have their own Twitter feed.

Perhaps inspired by gestures like Fénéon's, a group of Italian futurists in 1915 claimed: "It's stupid to write one hundred pages where one would do." It was advice that Ernest Hemingway would heed when he composed the shortest novel ever, consisting of six words—a mere thirty-three characters (spaces and punctuation included)—which he penned in the 1920s:

For sale: baby shoes, never worn.

Allegedly written on a lark as a bet among a group of drunken writers in a New York restaurant as to who could write a six-word novel, Papa scribbled his quickly down on a cocktail napkin and won. While it displays all of Hemingway's characteristic wit and brilliance, research has shown the story to be apocryphal. These words had been kicking around in various forms in newspapers and advertisements before Hemingway snagged them. In 1906, an ad read: "For sale, baby carriage; never been used. Apply at this office." And in 1912, another ad, perhaps inspired by the first, said: "Baby's hand made trousseau and baby's bed for sale. Never been used." Like a game of telephone, variations on this theme continued throughout the early twentieth century. Clearly, Hem—a newspaperman—dug into his vast mental knowledge of the field and, on the spot, reframed preworn ad copy, claiming it as an original—and brilliant—novel. Hemingway's gesture is a reminder that all language is preexisting and that smart recontextualization can often make used words new. On the web—an environment where language is cut and pastable—claiming originality is a tricky game. If you can think of it, it already exists on the Internet, which is why people often come up with the identical concept at the same time, a phenomenon known as multiple discovery. As the mathematician Farkas Bolyai noted: "When the time is ripe, these things appear in different places in the manner of violets coming to light in early spring."

In 2014, the visual artist Cory Arcangel published a book about procrastination called *Working On My Novel*, which was repurposed from his Twitter feed, which only retweeted tweets that contained the phrase "working on my novel." He then culled the best of them into a paperbound book. Each page contains one tweet:

> *Currently working on my novel*
> *and listen to really nice music.*
> *Yeah I'm a writer deal with it.*
> *Sierra Brown—1:25 AM—1 Dec 12*

I'm working on my novel again,
and it feels good, you guys. I love
my mind.
Stephen Mangol—11:44 PM —23 Sep 12

As Arcangel explains, "Part of the fun was that if you're twittering about how you're working on your novel, you're probably not working on your novel! I love these situations." What were they doing instead of writing? Wasting time on the Internet—which is exactly what Arcangel was doing when he wrote this book, though artists routinely waste time as part of their creative process, thereby cleverly and self-reflexively conflating procrastination with production.

In 2010, the Pulitzer Prize–winning fiction writer Jennifer Egan published an 8,500-word story consisting of tweets—one tweet a minute, in one-hour-daily bursts—over nine days on the *New Yorker* website. Although the text was written beforehand, Egan's story was as much about critiquing distribution—isn't Twitter supposed to be spontaneous?—as it was about what she was writing. But what she was writing was good: each tweet stands alone as a self-contained tweet, yet builds, tweet by tweet, into a narrative. Her Twitter novel begins:

People rarely look the way you expect them to, even when you've seen pictures.

The first thirty seconds in a person's presence are the most important.

If you're having trouble perceiving and projecting, focus on projecting.

Necessary ingredients for a successful projection: giggles; bare legs; shyness.

The goal is to be both irresistible and invisible.

It ends 607 tweets later with:

You won't know for sure until you see them crouching above you, their faces taut with hope, ready to jump.

Egan's twitter novel is a lovely rebuttal to Arcangel's book. She had actually been working on her novel for over a year, but then distributed it quickly and "spontaneously," blasted out in crystalline perfection over social media.

Since 2010, Steve Roggenbuck has been producing poetry that is made, distributed, and viewed almost exclusively on the web, taking the form of Facebook posts, YouTube videos, and image macros. He became best known for a series of videos that show Roggenbuck either in bare apartments or out in the forest, manically improvising poems that celebrate the cosmos and our place in it. In one video, he screams at a

gray sky: "Make something beautiful before you are dead . . .
Maybe you should stand in the rain! You're alive right now!"
But this ain't no tree hugger or Iron John. There's an intensity and an edge to his work verging on violence, which is
at once terrifying, hypnotic, and completely moving. Roggenbuck uses shaky handheld cameras, hazy inspirational
background music, and rough jump cuts. Purposely aping
the look of amateur videos strewn across YouTube, they are
meticulously crafted infomercials for poetry. In another video, Roggenbuck, with his boyish acned face, thick eyebrows,
and scruffy hair, stares intensely into the camera and asks:
"I'm interested in marketing, but I'm mainly interested in
marketing the moon. Do you love the light of the moon, sir?
And if you don't, can I convince you?"

Along with Tao Lin, Roggenbuck is one of the bright
stars of Alt Lit, an online writing community that emerged
in 2011 and harnesses the casual affect and jagged stylis-
tics of social media as the basis of their works—poems, stories, novels, tweets, and status updates. Its members have
produced a body of distinctive literature marked by direct
speech, expressions of aching desire, and wide-eyed sincerity.
("language is so cool. i can type out these shapes and you can
understand me," or "Yay! Dolphins are beautiful creatures
and will always have a wild spirit. I have been very lucky because I have had the awesome experience of swimming with
dolphins twice.") The poems and stories, published on blogs
and Twitter feeds, are usually written in the Internet ver-
nacular of lowercase letters, inverted punctuation, abundant

typos, and bad grammar. While other web-based poetry movements exploit appropriated text—cutting and pasting or scooping vast amounts of preexisting data—Alt Lit tends to use emo-heavy, homespun language that bears the urgency and candor of a status update; no sentiment is too trite to be repurposed as poetry.

This type of writing has deep roots, extending back to the cosmological visions of William Blake, through the direct observation poems of the imagists, the anti-art absurdities of Dada, and the nutty playfulness of surrealism. In the second half of the twentieth century, a major touchstone is the beats, particularly Allen Ginsberg's spontaneous mind poems, Jack Kerouac's unfiltered spew, and Gary Snyder's environmental consciousness. The concrete poet Aram Saroyan's purposely misspelled single-word poem "lighght" is a model for much of the wordplay that occurs here (gorgeous moments like the reimagining of the words "can,t" and "youuuuu"). But there's a punk-inspired outlaw energy rippling through much of the work here.

Alt Lit and its siblings Weird Twitter (a group of writers who abuse the platform's 140-character conventions) and Flarf (an early Internet poetry movement), cull poems that feel like the Internet itself, jammed with screen caps of Twitter updates, image macros, and photoshopped collages that appear between lineated verse, short stories, and blog entries.

One prominent Weird Twitter poet is Jacob Bakkila, then a BuzzFeed employee who between 2011 and 2013 wrote under the pseudonym of @Horse_ebooks, a feed that was widely presumed to have been written by a spambot. The feed was widely followed; people were charmed that a bot could've come up with lines like: "Their negativity only served to push me deeper into the realms of soap making" or "HOLY COW!! . . . DOG TOYS ARE GETTING EXPENSIVE WHY NOT." In 2013, Bakkila announced that the feed was indeed authored by him and that the project was finished. When @ Horse_ebooks was thought to be a machine, the misspellings, non sequiturs, and fractured sentences were charming, the by-products of an inferior literary "mind" whose struggle to get it right humanized it.

In his video "'AN INTERNET BARD AT LAST!!!' (ARS POETICA)," Roggenbuck talks about his debt to the past. "Five and a half years ago, I read Walt Whitman and it changed my life," he says. "Walt Whitman had made me appreciate my life more actively than I had ever appreciated it before. Walt makes you step back and say, the world is wonderful, this whole thing that is going on is wonderful. Pay attention to what is going on." Technology is the key. "The purpose of the Bard is my purpose," he says. "This is the dream for poets, to be a poet when the Internet exists. Man! We got an opportunity!" The video concludes with Roggenbuck connecting the past and present: "You know that Walt Whitman would die for this, that Walt Whitman would be on a TweetDeck, kicking his legs up, and going ha-a-a-ard."

The Revolution Will Be Mobilized

AT&T recently ran a series of ads promoting its merger with DirecTV that had the tagline: "The revolution will not only be televised, the revolution will be mobilized." One ad opens by showing various nighttime locations in New York City with lots of screens—places like Times Square and sports bars. At the same time the denizens of those locations are all glued to their mobile devices. It's a hyperconnected, super-distracted world; everyone is furiously multitasking, keeping one eye on their device and the other on the huge public screens. Suddenly, without warning, the screens glitch and go black. In the silent darkness, the camera pans across legions of bewildered and frightened faces that look up from their devices hoping for some explanation. Then, in another instant, the screens blink and flash back to life. The camera pans across the crowd, visibly relieved. Their smiling faces are now glued to the reactivated screens, which display clips from films like *The Matrix*, with Morpheus saying, "After this, there is no turning back." A user picks up his smartphone to find Mr. Spock proclaiming, "History is replete with turning points." A woman swipes a giant touch screen that displays a jubilant fist-pumping A-Rod, as a voice-over screams, "When fantasy becomes reality!" The ad ends with the final scene of *Casablanca*, projected on the skyscrapers of Wall Street: "Louie, I think this is the beginning of a beautiful friendship," ballyhooing the convergence of TV and mobile media. The future has arrived and it's better than we expected. In that one glitch, it's as if the entire world got a huge reboot into the future.

The ad, with its mix of hope, fear, and redemption, brought to mind the Y2K hysteria. Just past midnight in 2000 on that New Year's Eve when the world didn't end, my sister-in-law, a historian at Berkeley, explained to us that traditionally a moment of doubt occurs right before cultures fully embrace new circumstances. She compared the Y2K crisis to previous millennial frenzies, suggesting that our thousand-years' fears this time around were being displaced not on God, but on technology. She added that cycles of guilt, repentance, and grace often accompany such trials, which always turn out to be nothing more than fear-fueled mirages. The Y2K introspection was the final barrier to our full embrace of technology, which was collectively vanquished that evening. With the dawn of the new millennium, we were poised to move into— in the words spouted by a cartoon character on the AT&T ad—"The future, to the glorious future!"

The theorist Paul Virilio has a concept he calls the "integral accident," which says that every time a technology is invented, an accident is invented with it. So, when the ship is invented, you get a shipwreck; the train, a train wreck; the airplane, the plane crash. These early technological accidents impacted a geographically specific area: the woods where the plane went down was affected in isolation. But when it comes to electromagnetic waves, such as radiation from a nuclear accident, the results of that accident are no longer felt locally but have networked implications. When the Fukushima reactor melted down, the radiation traveling through the Pacific Ocean food chain endangered fish on the West Coast of America. Similarly, market meltdowns in China crash Western economies. A virus in an electronic network can act with devastating results, infecting many, not just one. The integral or whole accident moves from local to general.

Little did we know that a mere year and a half later, an older technology—airplanes—would engender an integral accident in ways that Y2K could not. On 9/11 in New York City, overloaded cell phone networks went dead and overtaxed sites like CNN.com and NYTimes.com refused to load. Subways, buses, and commuter trains—many of them controlled by computers—stopped running. The island was sealed off from the rest of the world, thrown back to the darkness of earlier times. Broadcast television for much of Manhattan was unavailable as the giant TV antennas atop the Twin Towers were no more. Like those screen-addled citizens in the AT&T ad, we sat there in the dark bereft of our devices, huddled close to our transistor radios trying to get the latest news as if it were the great New York City blackout of 1965. For the next week or two, our technology barely worked; even our data-driven stock markets went dark. Lower Manhattan, closed to vehicular traffic, resembled a cross between a nineteenth-century village and post-WWII Berlin. We languidly ambled down the great avenues as if they were country lanes, while in the background great plumes of acrid smoke spewed from the Lower West Side.

Without distraction from our technology, we rediscovered each other, looking into faces rather than screens, slowing down for person-to-person chats while we sat in silent parks, soaking in the glorious mid-September sunshine. There was an eerie silence in the city, one that was punctuated only by the frequent wailing of sirens. It was an escape from the stress of recent events, an enforced return to a lost time, but one that could not last. As the networks sprang back to life and the transportation began running again, we picked up right where we had left off, roaming the streets with Blackberrys glued to our palms, each in our own bubble. Over the next few years, crises like blackouts and hurricanes would plunge us back into darkness for short periods. These enforced digital detoxes became more harrowing than refreshing. During Hurricane Sandy, impromptu charging stations powered by generators sprung up on the streets, as groups of New Yorkers huddled together in the cold, waiting an eternity for their devices to charge before they headed back to their primitive dark caves.

AT&T's ads of course were riffs on Gil Scott-Heron's

1970 song "The Revolution Will Not Be Televised," which proclaimed that media would play absolutely no role in the forthcoming social and political revolutions that had begun in the 1960s. Forty-five years ago, Scott-Heron had seen how all experience had been influenced, framed, and saturated by media, robbing us, he felt, of our human experience. We had been turned into zombies, bent on consumerism and stripped of our political import. He was pleading for deprogramming, hoping we might reject media spectacles and instead take to the streets, where the revolution would happen away from the cameras, in "real time," where there would be no "instant replay." After all, if the urban riots of the 1960s showed anything, they demonstrated that highly technological civilizations could be plunged into darkness and chaos with basic means: the striking of a single match or the throwing of a Molotov cocktail. AT&T's snarky usurping of Scott-Heron's political message proclaimed total victory; corporate-sponsored technology was now a foregone conclusion and there would be no turning back. Ever. The future had arrived, and it looked an awful lot like Big Brother.

But the truth is more complex than that. AT&T's ads showed us a one-sided, oversimplistic, skewed vision of the "revolution." At a Black Lives Matter panel I attended recently called "The Fire This Time," an audience member asked why and how the movement emerged when it did. One of the panelists responded by simply reaching into his pocket and holding up his smartphone. In an unanticipated twist to both AT&T and Scott-Heron, the revolution is, in fact, both televised—uploaded to social media and replayed endlessly—and mobilized (people mobilized by mobile media) in the service of justice. The corporate technological apparatuses that Scott-Heron had so rightly feared had now been distributed among the citizenry to record trespasses that not long ago went unnoticed, able to bring light to the darkest and most unjust corners of the world. The fire this time is a digital flame, capable of illuminating darkness and torching unjust systems.

Many articles I read yearn for a return to solitude and introspection, quiet places far removed from the noises of our devices. But those places, away from the rabble of the street, are starting to remind me of gated communities: highly patrolled spaces where discourse is circumscribed and vetted. What they are ignoring is that for many communities, the presence of devices to record and distribute events that entrenched powers that be would rather not have anyone see, are tools of social justice, crucial to pointing out abuses of power. I read that our devices are removing us from life, but when a device records an injustice, it's an indicator of presence, not absence.

In another one of those AT&T ads, the line between presence and absence is obliterated as image after image is shown of people watching their devices while they are doing something else. A guy in a stuffy concert hall sneaks a peek at his smartphone while a voice-over decries: "Flip between the fight, the game, and the ballet you didn't want to go to!"; or someone sweating it out on a treadmill, phone in his hand: "Binge while you lose weight!"; a surfer in the curl of a wave: "Channel-surf while you surf!"; or a mountain climber dangling in midair: "Enjoy a good cliffhanger while you hang from a cliff!"

Like many, AT&T would like you to think we use our devices in one way only: to indulge in frivolous media while we are doing things we don't want to be doing. However, the truth is more complicated. Our use of media mimics our circadian rhythms, as we cycle through periods of being awake and being asleep. We are neither complete zombies, nor completely present: usually it's a mix of the two. The smartphone that captured the police shooting death of Walter Scott might have been, just a moment before, playing Candy Crush Saga, and right afterward, wasting time on the Internet.

APPENDIX

101 Ways to Waste Time
on the Internet

What follows is a set of ideas on how to waste time on the Internet. They were authored by my class in the initial offering of Wasting Time on the Internet at the University of Pennsylvania, January–April 2015.

1. Have one person browse the Internet while connected to a big monitor. A group stands behind that person loudly screaming what to click on. It would begin by one person at a time yelling commands: Click that link! Type this into the status update window! Then it gradually increases to a polyphonic cacophony of unbearable intensity.

2. Instagram something with the intention of it being taken down by Instagram. Take a screenshot of it; keep a record of it. Instagram the screenshot. Screenshot that Instagram. If it is taken down again, repeat the process

until all you're posting is a screenshot of a screenshot of a screenshot . . . of the original photo.

3. Sit in a circle and pass your laptop to the person next to you. For one minute, they can open anything on your computer. Once something is opened, it must be left opened. You may not alter or delete anything, just expose. At the end of one minute, you pass that laptop to the person on your left and they get one minute with it. By the time it arrives back to you, everyone will have had their turn with your laptop. Everything that people have opened will remain open on your screen for you to see.

4. Delete as much as you can from Facebook. Avoid deleting friends, and avoid deleting your account. Keep a tally and see among your friends who can delete the most.

5. In a group, skype a person not in the group. Refuse to answer any questions about why you did this.

6. In a partner's Facebook account, find their oldest message and who it was sent to or by. On your own account, message that person and have a conversation.

7. Go on Netflix, and look at the first suggestion for your Top Picks. If you've already seen it, then pick the next suggestion. Read a generic Wikipedia article about the show/movie, and write a Facebook status using what you've learned (develop an opinion or a question or a statement). The status should not mention that you haven't seen the show/movie. Tag at least one person in the status.

8. For a period of hours, record your face with your webcam as you use your computer. Choose a long enough

time span that you will forget the camera is on.

9. Delete your Facebook profile picture and leave it blank for as long as you can.

10. Attend a lecture, meeting, performance, meal, or movie and be on your smartphone the entire time.

11. Sit in a circle with a group and open your laptops. Plug your headphones into the computer to your right. Play music for your partner with this goal: Make the listening environment as annoying as possible. Play music the person hates. Play several songs at once.

12. Browse only using the earliest version of Internet Explorer you can find, for as long as you can. You may not close any pop-ups or tabs that appear.

13. In a group, sit in a circle with laptops. Plug your headphones into the laptop of the person to your left and play music for your partner. Let the vibes of the music your partner plays determine the next song you play for your partner. Try to get the circle to reach an equilibrium.

14. In a public place, have a partner receive instructions on their cell phone from the other partner sending them. Have the receiver do whatever the instructions say while the sender watches from the side.

15. Find a music mashup online and write a serious review of it as though you are a *New York Times* theater critic.

16. Post something to a friend's Facebook wall as if you were talking to someone else. Be as specific as you can.

17. Find a piece of audio you believe summarizes and represents the entire Internet.

18. Find a social media profile of someone you know or do not know and re-create their profile on your own page.

19. Make a dating profile for a partner and get them as many dates as you can.

20. On an online shopping website, attempt to fully re-create what you are wearing. Then find photos of other people wearing those clothes and collect them in a folder. In a group, compare to see who can find the most photos of their current outfit.

21. Take a resume from LinkedIn or an online resume sample site and apply for several jobs using this resume, as well as an online sample cover letter if one is required. Apply to these same jobs with your own resume and cover letter.

22. Display provocative captions on a projector and cycle through them quickly. Have a group post a Facebook status impulsively to each one.

23. Take a screenshot of as many viral YouTube videos as you can. Make a slideshow that displays the images as rapidly as possible.

24. Place a camera in a heavily used room. Make sure everyone who goes through the room is aware that the camera could record them, but that it may not. Covertly turn on and off the camera during the period of time.

25. Find a very public space, sit in a closed circle with your laptops. One person selects a video from Pornhub. At the count of three, everyone clicks on the video and watches it together.

26. Find your biggest fear on the Internet and send it to a friend.

27. Think of ten friends who have different ideas about the Internet than you. Send a message to each of them asking what there is to do on the Internet. See what they tell you to do. Do nothing until one of them responds, then do it as quickly as you can, and ask another. While waiting for responses, think about what you asked them, how you phrased it, and why some did and did not respond.

28. Watch people in a public area and write down their physical attributes as if you were writing a crime report. Then look online at public police postings to find a crime with a suspect description that matches yours. Determine if they committed the crime or not.

29. Take an article you vehemently disagree with, post it as your Facebook status, and then say how you align yourself with everything it's saying. Like this status. Share it. Post it on other people's walls. Do the same thing on Twitter.

30. Interview a person for six seconds using Vine. Do not tell them the interview will last six seconds.

31. In a group, play different songs from as many devices as you can. Try to write down what you can discern from the noise.

32. With a partner, watch a short video in turns with one both recording the other with a camera as well as taking notes on the other's affective response. Put the original video, and the two reaction videos side by side in a new video.

33. Find a room or space that is reserved by someone else. Convince them there was a booking error with the online system and that it is actually yours.

34. Collaboratively take turns reading from each member's Facebook feed. Write the lines into a document as a poem.

35. Spend hours writing a document with a group however you like, but delete it when anyone leaves or enters the room.

36. Find sites of relaxation on the Internet. Spend some time on these sites and relax. When you are done, find rain sound audio on YouTube and listen to it while you write about drowning. Keep writing and writing until you cannot write more. Then delete everything you have written and move on with your life.

37. Using Google Maps satellite view, stitch together a new city. Give it a name, and invent laws for it.

38. Use a screen recorder like QuickTime to record your computer screen as you browse the Internet for eight minutes. Call a friend on Skype and make sure that's included in there.

39. Using their publicly available online profile, create a fake obituary for someone you know.

40. In public, open a laptop and surf the Internet. Have a partner watch you and the way people respond to you and the way you respond to others.

41. Ask each other about passwords. Talk about how you picked your password. Ask how other people picked

their passwords. Share your password if you want and explain what you like and don't like about it.

42. Venmo $100 to the person to your right. They must then Venmo $100 to the person to their right and so on until your money goes full circle and returns to you.

43. Find a database of scary stories generated on the Internet. In a group, collaboratively write a new story by each taking deliberate lines from the database and stitching them together.

44. Ask as many people in a public place how happy they are, and graph happiness relative to location on Google Maps.

45. Find a Facebook friend and message as many of their friends as you can asking them what they think of your person.

46. Take a compatibility quiz online with a partner. Then, check your answers by comparing your compatibility to whether your zodiac signs are compatible.

47. Create an Instagram account and use whatever means necessary to get followers.

48. Find a YouTube video and make it viral.

49. Work in a group to invent a rumor. Spread the rumor on as many social media sites as possible.

50. Go on a video chat website like Omegle and ask people to put a shoe on their head. Share the screenshots.

51. Check out as many books as you can from a library. Compare how the information differs from commonly used websites on the same subjects.

52. Create a Twitter account that only posts lyrics from a specific lyricist. Do this for as many lyricists as you would like to get to know. Have each account follow each other, plus some other accounts of your choosing.

53. Open a text document and raid a partner's computer with as much text as you can from their personal files. Send your text document to your friends.

54. Clog as much as you can. Clog online forums for your school or work. Post a series of blank posts on your Face-book feed, send a bunch of blank e-mails to everyone you know, open a bunch of blank tabs, and just clog everything. CLOG. What does it feel like to apply force to the Internet?

55. Within the constraint of two hundred words, try to offend as many people as possible in a Facebook post.

56. Narrate the life story of the person across a table from you using only GIFs. Make it as long or short as you want but make sure to highlight what you think might have been key moments in that person's life or even better, make something up. Do not caption your work.

57. Snapchat your surroundings to a partner with the timer on one second. Send only one Snapchat each minute. Try to guess where the other person is.

58. Find the first friend you made on Facebook and have a conversation with them.

59. In a library, find someone who is wasting time on the Internet. Ask them what they are doing and what they would be doing if they were being productive.

60. Go to a random urban location on Google Street View. Share this with another person and see how long it takes them to determine the location. Consider what factored into the time and ultimate guess the person made.

61. Cross arms with people in a group and use your hands to type on the laptops in front of your left and right partners as they type on your own. Try to navigate.

62. Send a Snapchat to buddies of a partner but not to them.

63. Like twenty posts on a single person's Facebook wall from that person's account.

64. Plan the most expensive three-day vacation in the world to the dollar amount using travel websites.

65. Watch a video and consciously misinterpret it. Spread your misinterpretation as far as you can.

66. In a group, attempt to find the shortest route from one Wikipedia article to another by clicking on links in the page.

67. Generate a random phrase using an online generator. For every letter in the phrase, find a song that begins with that letter. Compile the results into a playlist named after your phrase.

68. Write a travel review for a trip you didn't take. Post it, then delete it and reflect on the memory of your trip.

69. In a group, have one person choose two behavior rules. Distribute one rule to all but one of the other members of the group, and the other to only one. Make it discreet so you do not know who got the majority rule and who

got the minority. In a chat room, have everyone type and act according to the rule they were given. See if the majority can identify the minority and vice versa, and if they can determine each other's rules.

70. Take as many pictures of the room you are in as possible. Upload the pictures to social media. Consider new ways to capture a space to re-create it elsewhere.

71. Pick a genre of music you don't usually listen to or that you dislike. Listen to five minutes of it without doing anything else. Once you pick a song, you have to listen to the whole thing. Don't touch the computer as you listen. After the five minutes, write about what you felt/were thinking about. How did it feel to do nothing but listen to something you don't like?

72. Charge fifteen people publicly on Venmo for $0.01–$3,000 for reasons you make up.

73. Exchange phones with a partner and text someone from that phone whatever you feel like.

74. In a group, choose one person to be the "gimp," so to speak. This person must have every avenue (social media, e-mail, different chat programs such as Skype, Google Chat, Canvas, etc.) Flood this person with as much spam as possible. Do what you will. The victim must copy and paste every message into a Word document.

75. Give your Facebook password to a partner and have them delete your account.

76. Open three video chat platforms at once and talk to three separate people.

77. Skype a buddy during one class for the whole class. Have the video chat muted but talk to them through text the entire class.

78. Sit down in the middle of a crowded walkway and open your laptop to surf the Internet.

79. Click on a spam advertisement and try to claim whatever promotion it's offering. Get yourself that iPhone for $20 or a free $100 Walmart gift card.

80. Look through your Facebook messages and go back as far as you can. Find the oldest message to which you never responded. Write back. Make the responses really long and detailed. Make it super awkward. Don't explain why you're writing back now or apologize for not writing back earlier.

81. Open an image on a screen and use as many devices as you can to iteratively take a picture of that image. Use as many people and as many cameras as you can, but plan it so that it takes the shortest amount of time for the image to travel from the first screen to the last. Configure the cameras and screen in physical space cleverly to do this.

82. Send as many people as you can lyrics from a song. Keep sending them even if people ask you to stop.

83. Using TV Trope, describe the people around you as tropes from the website.

84. Graffiti the Facebook wall of the person to your left. Post anything you want and everything you want. Vandalize it. Make it so their grandmas on Facebook call them asking what's wrong.

85. As a group, choose a popular album of music. Find the worst possible versions of each song on the web, be it a terrible cover on YouTube, a bad quality download, a virus-laden download, a misheard lyrics version, or a horrible remix. Reconstruct the album out of these new versions.

86. Choose a partner and flood their social media accounts with the phrase "I love you" as many times and in as many specific places as possible. The partner must respond to each instance with the phrase "I love you too" as quickly as they can. Repeat with "I hate you."

87. Go onto ChatRoulette or Omegle and try to get people to tell you a secret. Post it to YouTube.

88. Find an interesting person in a different country and completely re-create their social media profile through your own Facebook. Proceed to comment on ten posts on your newsfeed only in that person's native language. If you don't know their language, that's even better: use Google Translate.

89. Join a chat room anonymously and admit as many secrets as you can.

90. Ask everyone around you to send you a picture of themselves they haven't posted online.

91. In a group, have everyone put their addresses in a bowl in the middle and each person draws one at random. Go on eBay and buy that person a present for less than one dollar.

92. In a public place, record the noise you hear with your

phone. Then go to a silent private place and listen to it. Send the noise to a partner and ask them where they think it is from.

93. Using Google Patent Search, find schematics of interesting devices. Post them to Instagram with a description in which you hashtag every other word.

94. In a group, select a person to take notes on the emotions, facial tics, and affects of a group of users surfing the Internet.

95. Find a niche piece of media that you love and find a place on the Internet where people are discussing it as recently as a month ago.

96. Delete a photo from the phone of a partner and do not tell them which you deleted.

97. Do a background check on the person to your left. Find every detail about them: addresses, schools, e-mail, hobbies, groups, publications, work, criminal record, family members, etc. Find everything you can by any means necessary. Hack into their accounts if necessary. Save what you find in a document. Send it to them.

98. For fifteen minutes, see who can tally the largest dollar amount by putting things in their Amazon shopping cart. The one with the most at the end of the time wins. Delete everything in your cart. Or don't.

99. Delete any document on your partner's computer. Don't tell them which one you erased. Then give them your laptop and have them do the same to you.

100. Make a website and fill it with spam.

101. Make a BuzzFeed account and post lists of how you waste time on the Internet.

Compiled by Chase Harrow. Contributors: Alan Chelak, Nina Friend, Chase Harrow, Bree Jackson, Melissa Kantrowitz, Justin Sheen, Parker Stakoff, Zoe Stoller, Patrick del Valle, John Vella, and Feimei Zeng.

ACKNOWLEDGMENTS

Portions of these chapters appeared in Ausgabe, the *Los Angeles Review of Books*, the *New Yorker*, the Poetry Foundation, Rhizome, Schwa Fire, and the *Wire*. In addition, sections of this book were presented live or excerpted from publications at the following venues: Fachhochschule Nordwestschweiz FHNW Basel, Transmediale, Kunsthaus Graz, LABOR, the Liverpool Biennial, MaMa Zagreb, Museum of Contemporary Art Barcelona, the Museum of Modern Art, the Institute of Fine Arts–NYU, Ràdio Web MACBA, the RISD Museum, the University of Cincinnati, and the Wattis Institute. I wish to thank the editors and the institutions for their support.

To my reader, critic, advisor, and lifelong companion, Cheryl Donegan, without whom this book would not exist. Special thanks to my agent, Paul Bresnick, and to my editors at HarperCollins, Barry Harbaugh and Eric Meyers as well as to Paula Cooper Hughes for her thoughtful insights on this book. I'd also like to thank Laura Beiles, Vicki Bennett, Claire Bishop, the Center for Programs in Contemporary Writing at the University of Pennsylvania, Roc Jiménez de Cisneros, Kathleen Donegan, Pamela Echeverria, Frenchie Ferenczi, Al Filreis, Henriette Gallus, Rainer Ganahl, David Haglund, Pablo Helguera, Sheila Heti, Katia Huemer, Jean Boite Éditions, Grant Jenkins, Shea Matthew Kennisher, Marcell Mars, Chus Martinez, Tomislav Medak, Ingo Niermann, Peter Pakesch, Lucrecia Palacios, Anna Ramos, Mingo Reynolds, Marisol Rodriguez, Agustin Pérez Rubio, Dubravka Sekuli , Arjan Singh, Caleb Smith, Danny Snelson, Sasha Weiss, Terry Winters, and Wendy Woon. And finally a huge shoutout to the students of UPenn's ENG 165 who tested, challenged, confirmed, and refined many of the ideas in this book.

ENDNOTES

INTRODUCTION: LET'S GET LOST

1   "nuclear deal with Iran": http://www.nytimes.com/2015/07/15/opinion/thomas-friedman-obama-makes-his-case-on-iran-nuclear-deal.html, August 17, 2015.

5   "talking cure": http://www.nytimes.com/2015/09/27/opinion/sunday/stop-googling-lets-talk.html, October 12, 2015.

8   "books are vanishing": http://www.slate.com/blogs/behold/2015/01/09/reinier_gerritsen_photographs_readers_on_the_subway_in_his_series_the_last.html, March 15, 2016.

8   "the vested interests": Excerpt from: Marshall McLuhan, *Understanding Media* (New York: McGraw-Hill, 1965), unpaginated, iBooks.

14 "I don't have a lot of time" : Michael Barbaro and Steve Eder. "Under Oath, Donald Trump Shows His Raw Side." *New York Times*, July 28, 2015, p. A1.

15 "the content of writing": McLuhan, *Understanding Media*.

15 "merely the sum of my posts": http://www.nytimes.com/2015/07/12/travel/going-off-the-grid-on-a-swedish-island.html, July 12, 2015.

18 "a security blanket": http://www.nytimes.com/2015/07/12/sunday-review/addicted-to-your-phone-theres-help-for-that.html, July 12, 2015.

18 "and yet in psychoanalytic theory": https://thinkingthoughtsdotorg.wordpress.com/2013/05/14/d-w-winnicott-on-transitional-object-and-transitional-space/, July 12, 2015.

24 "a tissue of quotations": http://www.ubu.com/aspen/aspen5and6/threeEssays.html#barthes, January 14, 2016.

CHAPTER 1: THE SOCIAL NETWORK

29 "we spend our lives in front of screens": https://www.english. upenn.edu/courses/undergraduate/2015/spring/engl111.301, January 17, 2016.

40 "the figure of the ghost": http://www.theguardian.com/books/ booksblog/2011/jun/17/hauntology-critical, December 31, 2015.

CHAPTER 2: THE WALKING DEAD

50 "they are such a pervasive and insistent part of daily life": http://www.washingtonpost.com/business/technology/ supreme-court-cellphone-ruling-hints-at-broader-curbs- on-surveillance/2014/06/25/2732b532-fc9b-11e3–8176- f2c941cf35f1_story.html, October 13, 2015.

51 "I believe in the future resolution": http://www.poetryfounda- tion.org/bio/andre-breton, January 17, 2016.

51 "every day they want to spend": Ruth Brandon. *Surreal Lives.* New York: Grove Press, 1999, 201.

52 "when will we have sleeping logicians": André Breton. *Mani- festos of Surrealism.* Ann Arbor: University of Michigan Press, 1969, 12.

55 "walking, then, is an act of reading": Michel de Certeau. *The Practice of Everyday Life.* Berkeley: University of California, 1984.

57 "I'm struggling with my picture": Mark Stevens and Anna- lyn Swan. *De Kooning: An American Master.* New York: A. A. Knopf, 2004.

60 "search for encrypted": http://www.adweek.com/socialtimes/ social-media-newsfeed-edward-snowden-on-social-media- twitter-isis-threats/206133, October 13, 2015.

65 "the warmth of a seat": http://www.dada-companion.com/ duchamp/archive/duchamp_walking_on_infrathin_ice.pdf, October 29, 2015.

65 "optimistic, futuristic": http://www.sfgate.com/default/ article/Q-and-A-With-Brian-Eno-2979740.php, July 25, 2015.

69 "look at those images objectively": http://www.wired.com/2012/04/an-essay-on-the-new-aesthetic/, October 13, 2015.

72 "odd gestures of any kind": Paul Auster. "Fogg in the Park" in *Central Park: An Anthology*. Ed. Andrew Blauner. New York: Bloomsbury, 2012, 101–2.

72 "in big cities, beneath the roar of traffic": http://www.nytimes.com/2015/09/26/nyregion/pope-francis-visits-new-york-city.html, October 29, 2015.

CHAPTER 3: OUR BROWSER HISTORY IS THE NEW MEMOIR

78 "I do a lot of exercises": William Burroughs and Brion Gysin. *The Third Mind*. New York: Seaver Books/Viking, 1978, 1.

82 "mindfulness in its original Buddhist tradition": http://op-talk.blogs.nytimes.com/2014/06/30/the-mindfulness-backlash/?_r=0, August 14, 2015.

83 "it's not that what is past casts its light": Walter Benjamin. *The Arcades Project*. Cambridge: Harvard University Press, 1999, 462, N2a,3.

84 "to compress all the possibilities": Raoul Hausmann. "Manifesto of PREsentism" in *Manifesto: A Century of ISMs*. Ed. Mary Ann Caws. Lincoln: University of Nebraska Press, 2001, 164.

84 "memory is not an instrument for exploring": Walter Benjamin. *Selected Writings*. Cambridge, Mass.: Belknap Press of Harvard University Press, 2004, 661.

86 "studies show that most people happily use the web": https://kasperskycontenthub.com/usa/files/2015/06/Digital-Amnesia-Report.pdf, September 7, 2015.

88 "there is a definite relationship between inertia": John Armitage. "From Modernism to Hypermodernism and Beyond: An Interview with Paul Virilio." *Theory Culture and Society* 16 (1999): 40.

CHAPTER 4: ARCHIVING IS THE NEW FOLK ART

90 "if that's real": Deborah Bright. "Shopping the Leftovers:

Warhol's Collecting Strategies in *Raid the Icebox*" in *Art History* 24 (2001): 2.

93 "the grid announces": Rosalind E. Krauss. *The Originality of the Avant-garde and Other Modernist Myths*. Cambridge, Mass: MIT Press, 1986, 9.

95 "boyhood bug collection": http://www.theguardian.com/technology/2014/apr/05/pinterest-interview-ben-silbermann-social-media, January 5, 2015.

96 "among children, collecting is only one process of renewal": Walter Benjamin. "Unpacking My Library" in *Walter Benjamin: Selected Writings. 1931–1934. Vol. 2. Pt. 2.* Cambridge: Belknap Press of Harvard University Press, 2004, 488.

96 "catalog of ideas": http://phys.org/news/2015–07-pinterest-ceo-site-future-ideas.html, January 8, 2015.

96 "if there is a counterpart": Benjamin, "Unpacking My Library," 487.

97 "adults and children": John Berger. *Ways of Seeing*. London: Penguin Books, 1972, 30.

98 "like everything else [curating] has been democratized": "Hans Ulrich Obrist interviews STEWART BRAND." Undated. Unpublished. E-mailed to author by Obrist, June 15, 2015.

99 "you have read all these books": Benjamin, *Selected Writings*, 71.

99 "even if all knowledge": Ann M. Blair. *Too Much to Know: Managing Scholarly Information before the Modern Age*. New Haven: Yale University Press, 2010, 5.

99 "sheer cognitive exhaustion": Ibid., 5.

100 "$10 billion": http://www.slate.com/articles/technology/technology/2013/01/aaron_swartz_jstor_mit_can_honor_the_internet_activist_by_fighting_to_make.html, February 17, 2013.

101 "range of arcane subjects": http://www.huffingtonpost.com/2013/02/11/philip-parker-books_n_2648820.html, October 22, 2015.

102 "Iraq War alone": https://en.wikipedia.org/wiki/WikiLeaks, July 22, 2013.

102 "United States diplomatic cable leaks": https://en.wikipedia.

org/wiki/United_States_diplomatic_cables_leak, July 22, 2013.

102 "there's a principle that says": http://blog.foreignpolicy.com/posts/2010/11/28/has_wikileaks_finally_gone_too_far, July 22, 2013.

103 "and with every new leak": http://www.newsweek.com/how-much-did-snowden-take-not-even-nsa-really-knows-253940, October 23, 2015.

103 "if recorded": http://www.davidzwirner.com/wp-content/uploads/2011/10/2009-OK-DZ-press-release.pdf, August 29, 2015.

104 "Philosophical Transactions": http://pirateproxy.ca/torrent/6554331, July 22, 2013.

106 "it feels like the end": Darren Wershler. E-mail to author, February 24, 2013.

108 "LABOR, UbuWeb, and Kenneth Goldsmith": http://printingtheInternet.tumblr.com/post/54177453547/proposal, September 10, 2013.

109 "please don't print the Internet": http://www.change.org/petitions/please-don't-print-the-Internet, September 10, 2013.

109 "Know Your Meme": http://knowyourmeme.com/memes/events/printing-out-the-Internet, August 30, 2015.

111 "the composition of vast books": Jorge Luis Borges. *Ficciones*. New York: Grove Press, 1962, 15.

112 "THE ARTIST MAY CONSTRUCT": http://ubu.com/papers/weiner_statements.html, September 17, 2013.

112 "in conceptual art the idea or concept": http://emerald.tufts.edu/programs/mma/fah188/sol_lewitt/paragraphs%20on%20conceptual%20art.htm, September 17, 2013.

113 "do not forget that a poem": Ludwig Wittgenstein. *Zettel*. Ed. G. E. M. Anscombe and G. H. von Wright, Berkeley: University of California Press, 1967, sec. 160.

CHAPTER 5: DREAM MACHINES AND ETERNIDAYS

116 "a kind of curator of culture": Deborah Solomon. *Utopia Park-*

way: The Life and Work of Joseph Cornell. New York: Farrar, Straus and Giroux, 1997, 359.

117 "three thousand books": Lynda Roscoe Hartigan. "Joseph Cornell's Dance with Duality" in *Joseph Cornell: Shadowplay Eterniday.* New York and London: Thames and Hudson, 2003, 15.

120 "everybody should have two television sets": Joseph Gelmis. "Andy Warhol" in *I'll Be Your Mirror.* Ed. Kenneth Goldsmith. New York: Carroll and Graf, 2004, 166.

121 "the distracted person is not just absent": http://quod.lib. umich.edu/cgi/t/text/text-idx?cc=mqr;c=mqr;c=mqrarchive; idno=act2080.0048.410;rgn=main;view=text;xc=1;g=mqrg, September 21, 2015.

122 "this extension of [Narcissus]": McLuhan, *Understanding Media.* unpaginated iBooks.

127 "I am the first to be surprised and often terrified": https:// www.moma.org/learn/moma_learning/1168–2, January 19, 2016.

129 "today, no exhibition is complete": Claire Bishop. "Digital Divide." *Artforum*, September 2010, 436.

129 "noticed his hands": Solomon, *Utopia Parkway*, 244.

131 "Harry Jay Knowles is sprawled on the edge of his bed": http://www.nytimes.com/1997/11/16/magazine/the-two-hollywoods-harry-knowles-is-always-listening.html?page-wanted=all, August 3, 2015.

132 "I was their experiment": http://www.hollywoodreporter.com/ news/aint-cools-harry-knowles-cash-430734, July 23, 2015.

133 "a contemporary brain": Lynda Roscoe Hartigan. *Joseph Cornell: Shadowplay Eterniday.* London: Thames and Hudson, 2003, 25.

135 "ultimate work of appropriation art": http://www.nytimes. com/2011/02/04/arts/design/04marclay.html?_r=0, April 11, 2016

136 "if you make something good": http://www.newyorker.com/mag-azine/2012/03/12/the-hours-daniel-zalewski, April 11, 2016

138 "a commons to which all humanity is entitled": Jonathan Crary.

24/7: Late Capitalism and the Ends of Sleep. iBooks.

139 "light from other days": Hartigan. *Joseph Cornell*, 2003, 148.

CHAPTER 6: I SHOOT THEREFORE I AM

145 "in the case of Instagram": http://www.cnbc.com/2015/09/23/instagram-hits-400-million-users-beating-twitter.html, January 19, 2016.

149 "perhaps part of the beauty": E-mail to author, October 12, 2015.

151 "we protest against": http://www.notbored.org/generic.jpg, October 11, 2015.

154 "given its cultural significance": http://www.theguardian.com/artanddesign/photography-blog/2014/jun/13/photoshop-first-image-jennifer-in-paradise-photography-artefact-knoll-dullaart, August 10, 2015.

154 "the world was young": http://rhizome.org/editorial/2013/sep/5/letter-jennifer-knoll/, August 10, 2015.

154 "a fake painting": Susan Sontag, *On Photography*. New York: RosettaBooks, 1973/2005, 66.

155 "a writer could not do that": Mel Gussow. *Conversations with Beckett*. New York: Grove Press, 2001, 47.

156 "Jennifer in Photoshop": http://jennifer.ps/, October 29, 2015.

156 "the beauty of the Internet": http://www.theguardian.com/artanddesign/photography-blog/2014/jun/13/photoshop-first-image-jennifer-in-paradise-photography-artefact-knoll-dullaart, August 10, 2015.

158 "what Prince is doing": http://www.huffingtonpost.com/2015/05/27/richard-prince-instagram_n_7452634.html, September 19, 2015.

158 "once you have shared User Content": https://help.instagram.com/155833707900388, October 29, 2015.

162 "the two propositions": Ludwig Wittgenstein. *Philosophy and Language*. London: Routledge, 1972, 304.

162 "*Google, Volume 1*": http://www.jean-boite.fr/box/google-volume-1, April 11, 2016.

163 *"I'm Google"*: http://dinakelberman.tumblr.com/, January 5, 2016.

163 "results visually in a colorful grid": http://dinakelberman.tumblr.com/, December 31, 2015.

166 "a history which the museum": Fred Wilson (med.). "Services: Working-Group Discussions." *October* 80 (Spring 1997): 117–48.

166 "not for sex": http://www.villagevoice.com/2007–02–13/art/critiqueus-interruptus/, viewed November 15, 2011.

CHAPTER 7: LOSSY AND JAGGY

170 "5 percent": http://www.wired.com/2012/02/why-neil-young-hates-mp3-and-what-you-can-do-about-it/, October 11, 2015.

170 "we live in the digital age": Ibid.

172 "The Ghost in the MP3": http://theghostinthemp3.com/, April 11, 2016

173 "MP3s' sizzle" http://radar.oreilly.com/2009/03/the-sizzling-sound-of-music.html, July 14, 2015.

173 "iPhone actually won out": http://appleinsider.com/articles/15/02/02/neil-youngs-400-pono-hi-def-music-player-loses-to-apples-iphone-in-blind-audio-test, July 14, 2015.

174 "streaming has ended for me": https://www.facebook.com/NeilYoung/posts/10155765667375317:0, August 8, 2015.

175 "discarded 35 mm movie film" Lev Manovich. *The Language of New Media*. Cambridge, Mass.: MIT Press, 2002, 47.

177 "twenty-three million animated GIFs": http://www.nytimes.com/2015/08/04/technology/gifs-go-beyond-emoji-to-express-thoughts-without-words.html?_r=0, October 11, 2015.

177 "five million animations": Ibid.

179 "due to its high compression rates": https://en.wikipedia.org/wiki/High-definition_video, January 17, 2016.

179 "In the class society of imagery": Hito Steyerl. "In Defense of the Poor Image" in *The Wretched of the Screen*. Berlin: Sternberg Press, 2012, 33.

180 "The poor image is a rag or a rip": Ibid., 32.

180 "perfect cinema—technically and artistically": http://www.ejumpcut.org/archive/onlinessays/JC20folder/ImperfectCinema.html, July 18, 2015.

181 "this is precisely why": Steyerl, "In Defense of the Poor Image," 42.

181 "Whereas before, a chosen few produced images": http://www.e-flux.com/journal/the-weak-universalism/, July 18, 2015.

182 "worst possible quality JPEGS": http://www.foto8.com/live/thomas-ruff-interview/, July 19, 2015.

183 "How much visual information": http://www.anothermag.com/art-photography/1840/thomas-ruff, July 19, 2015.

CHAPTER 8: THE WRITER AS MEME MACHINE

192 "This ethos is evident": http://thejogging.tumblr.com/, September 9, 2015.

200 "commit to making every message": http://five.sentences/, August 3, 2015.

201 "We holler these trysts": http://www.poetryfoundation.org/poem-alone/241332?iframe=true, January 20, 2016.

208 "Responding to a call at night": Félix Fénéon. *Novels in Three Lines*. New York: New York Review of Books, 2007.

209 "It's stupid to write one hundred pages": F. T. Marinetti, Emilio Settimelli, and Bruno Corra. "The Futurist Synthetic Theatre": in *Manifesto, ISMs*. Ed. Mary Ann Caws. Lincoln: University of Nebraska Press, 2001, 695.

209 "For sale: baby shoes": https://en.wikipedia.org/wiki/For_sale:_baby_shoes,_never_worn, November 30, 2015.

210 "Currently working on my novel": http://www.vice.com/read/working-on-my-novel-cory-arcangel-interview-124, November 30, 2015.

211 "Part of the fun": http://www.bookforum.com/review/13895, November 30, 2015.

211 "People rarely look the way you expect them": http://www.newyorker.com/magazine/2012/06/04/black-box-2, November 30, 2015.

ABOUT THE AUTHOR

Kenneth Goldsmith is a conceptual artist, and the first poet laureate of the Museum of Modern Art. He is the author of *Seven American Deaths and Disasters* and the book of essays *Uncreative Writing*, breaking down the art form he pioneered. Goldsmith teaches at the University of Pennsylvania, where he taught the controversial Wasting Time on the Internet class that inspired this book. He lives in New York with artist Cheryl Donegan and their two sons.

Praise for *Wasting Time*

"For decades, Kenneth Goldsmith has forced us to question what constitutes and what does not constitute art. In *Wasting Time on the Internet*, he performs a crucial intellectual act, demonstrating persuasively and precisely the myriad ways in which the web undergirds contemporary art and ambitious contemporary art engages seriously with the implications of the web."

—David Shields, author of *Reality Hunger: A Manifesto*

"The Internet made the world an intelligence and vastly increased my own. I got my theory from Hawthorne's *House of the Seven Gables*, Wells's *World Brain*, and McLuhan, but now I have the Internet instruct… a pretty good histor…

—Glenn O'Bri…

"Face it: You alre… But Kenneth Gol… thinking about what we're all going to do anyway. Deeply versed in avant-garde and surreal modes of seeing and playing in the so-called 'real world,' he proves a brilliant guide to the worlds we describe as digital or virtual. And insights aside, it's pure pleasure to browse and surf and swipe and poke at contemporary tech culture in his company."

—Rob Walker, coeditor *Significant Objects*

"I have been a fan of Kenneth Goldsmith ever since I read his mind-boggling *Soliloquy* over a decade ago. Respected and reviled for doing the 'wrong thing at the wrong time,' he returns here with a rebuke to the popular notion that we're losing something important—intellectually, socially, and, as readers and thinkers—in this age of too much, too fast. I read it feeling offended, anxious, liberated, and gleeful."

—Sheila Heti, author of *How Should a Person Be?*

ALSO BY KENNETH GOLDSMITH